WHAT EVERY DREAM MEANS

To Kevin,
All the Best

WHAT EVERY DREAM MEANS

BY

SCOTT M SHAFER

Bookstand Publishing
www.BookstandPublishing.com

Published by
Bookstand Publishing
Gilroy, CA 95020
Record 2116_8

Scripture taken from the Holy Bible, King James Version

Cover Photography

Cover Design by Ty Walsworth
www.TyWalsworth.com

978-1-58909-463-5

Printed in the United States of America

Love unto all the saints, cease not to give thanks for you, making mention of you in my prayers; That the God of our Lord Jesus Christ, the Father of glory, may give unto you the spirit of wisdom and revelation in the knowledge of him: The eyes of your understanding being enlightened; that ye may know what is the hope of his calling, and what the riches of the glory of his inheritance in the saints, And what is the exceeding greatness of his power to us-ward who believe, according to the working of his mighty power, Which he wrought in Christ, when he raised Him from the dead, and set Him at his own right hand in the heavenly places, Far above all principality, and power, and might, and dominion, and every name that is named, not only in this world, but also in that which is to come: And hath put all things under His feet, and gave Him to be the head over all things to the church, which is His body, the fullness of Him that filleth all in all.

Ephesians 1:15b-23

ACKNOWLEDGEMENTS

This book is a first for me and hopefully something that will help aid in the process of changing the current paradigm among leaders in the body of Christ about dreams and night visions and their relevance today. It is not intended to be an exhaustive study of dreams but rather offers practical insight and idea's to help those interested in the topic. My hope is simply to plant seeds and to impart the Spirit of God, who is the ultimate source of a greater depth of understanding of dreams, night visions and their meaning for our lives. I want to first thank those who have prayed and encouraged me in this process of writing. Though others don't see your labors, I am grateful and extend my gratitude for you and your service to God. I want to thank Denice Johnson for your work on the final stages of the manuscript. Finally, I want to thank and honor above all, the one true source of all light and understanding, Jesus Christ.

CONTENTS

INTRODUCTION

Worldviews & Paradigms

PARADIGMS ARE POWERFUL. They create a lens through which we view various aspects of the spiritual life. As you read this book, my hope and prayer is that you would experience a divinely given paradigm of dreams, night visions, how they are interpreted and their relevance today. In this process of change in our thinking, it is important first to understand what paradigm we have previously had and the influences that may have shaped this old paradigm, before we begin to move toward a new paradigm. Let's first explore the meaning of this word paradigm and look at where it originated.

The word *paradigm,* dating from the 15th Century, came from Latin and Greek root words and was originally used as a scientific term. It was used to describe a philosophical or theoretical framework of a scientific school or discipline within which theories, laws, and generalizations and the experiments performed in support of them are formulated. Today it is more commonly used to mean "a model" or "a pattern" or an outstandingly clear or typical archetype. A *paradigm* then proceeds or originates from one's theories, and assumptions, or pertaining to ones perception, or frame of reference regarding a particular matter: not in terms of visual seeing but rather in terms of how we perceive, understand and interpret them.

In order to move toward a new paradigm with regards to dreams and night visions, this transition may require that we break with tradition or traditional mindsets and break with old ways of thinking based on prior knowledge (or lack thereof). It is to have a radically new view of the work of the Spirit and its application to our lives and in our understanding of the kingdom of God.

One major problem today is the sheer lack of practical, biblically based material written on dreams, night visions, and dream interpretation. There is very little instruction available that is written from a clear perspective of hearing God's voice, in order to feed this generation's spiritual hunger for understanding the ways of God and the things of the Spirit, including dreams and night visions.

Contemporary Thought

Most modern Christian authors avoid the subject of dream interpretation altogether. Unfortunately, others approach the topic from an unbiblical mixture of beliefs and perspectives that elicits a secular or humanistic mindset. Some writers today blend their formal psychological training which in essence is rooted in a Freudian and Jungian methodology and theory of dream interpretation with isolated biblical texts to support their opinion and viewpoints. At best this blend creates a complex yet diluted form of dream interpretation that is not grounded in scripture or in the concept of an intimate relationship with the living God. These interpretive theories fall short or miss the mark of those practiced by the true biblical dream interpreters of old, such as Daniel and Joseph the Patriarch.

These authors' purposes are very different from what the scriptures declare about God's purposes for dreams and night visions. Their primary intent is to understand the so-called subconscious mind or hidden aspects of one's personality. Though I appreciate the attempt to heal and understand various aspects of humanity, their diluted expression is severely limited and doesn't even compare or come close to the original or root intention of why God uses dreams to speak to people in scripture. In fact, for many, this change of focus has twisted, and quite possibly even obscured the whole concept of the gift and process of interpreting dreams from a godly perspective. Call me a purist if you will, but I want the real thing as I'm sure you do.

I believe the gift or anointing for interpreting dreams is quite rare in its mature form today in the church. The lack of instruction needed to achieve maturity is missing and this contributes to its lack of credibility overall. Thankfully, paradigms are slowly beginning to change as we're seeing a resurgence of interest and further study on dreams by prophets and teachers, and even apostolic figures across the body of Christ in some circles

Counting the Cost

For some time now, God has created within me a passion to help people gain an understanding of how significant dreams and night visions really are for all who receive them. It has come at a price; including years of misunderstanding and ridicule, sometimes even from those closest to me. Some of these struggles have come to develop my character, but yet others are due to the prophetic nature of dreams and visions. For example, consider the Patriarch Joseph and years of suffering and separation from his family.

It is my desire to see others become ignited with this same passion to understand and appreciate deeply this multi-faceted dimension of God's grace and His unfolding redemptive purpose in the earth during the last days. But we must understand that like many things of God, this passion is not without cost. It is my conviction that God is deeply interested in our sanctification and character development in order to get us to a point where we are trustworthy in His eyes. With all the gifts of the Holy Spirit we must be motivated by love (*1 Corinthians 13*). This love sets us free from the contamination of the most corrosive and damaging element of life; the corruption of pride in our hearts and minds. The apostle Peter stated it this way,

And all of you clothe yourselves with humility toward one another, for God is opposed to the proud, but gives grace to the humble.

1Peter 5:5

Counterfeits

Like so many other gifts of the Spirit, Satan has tried to counterfeit dream interpretation. In doing so he has successfully surrounded the realm of dreams with doubt and confusion. The enemy is well aware of the seven spirits of God, or these seven burning lamps before the throne of God (*Isaiah 11:2; Revelation 4:5*), including the Spirit of knowledge and understanding. Therefore, the deceiver has sought to discredit, devalue, and distort the power and validity of this 'Spirit' of understanding (*Isaiah 11:2)* and its operation within the realm of Christ-centered dream interpretation. Satan has tried to veil this gift throughout history especially in periods of intellectualism, including today's postmodern philosophical quagmire. We need to see clearly the perversion and deception that is in some contemporary interpreters in this field today, who are unfortunately quite prolific. I can't warn or express strongly enough just how devaluing their approach to dream interpretation is for the Christian.

My goal prayerfully is to help recover and restore what I believe is a part of the destiny of the people of God in these last days. I do not presume to be the only one called to do this. But I intend to be a voice in the overall process of restoration. I want to explore all that the Lord has done for us as His people. Dream interpretation is part of our inheritance as the people of God. We must take hold of it and I would be the first to admit that we must express it in its fully mature form, recovering this ancient practice that has been long lost and forgotten. We must respectfully insist upon it before God. With resolve we must insist on having dream interpretation in the midst of our gatherings, cultivating it in our own personal lifestyle and as well utilizing it in our evangelistic efforts. We do this by creating an environment for it. We must continue growing in it (yes, there is a growth process involved) and taking it back from Satan by sanctifying it for God's glory and redemptive purposes for the last day's church.

As I previously alluded to, we must be creative in using dream interpretation to win the lost and minister to pre-Christians in every place of influence we find ourselves, from friends and family to government and business relationships and so on. This is why it is vital to change the current paradigm to one that is truly biblical and illuminated by the Holy Spirit. We must change our minds before we can be effective and seize the opportunity that is before us in this time in history.

Identifying the Flaw

For this shift in our mindset to occur, we need to identify and rid ourselves of the flawed insights that the counterfeit or false dream interpreters offer those who are sincerely searching for answers from God. This is my purpose in identifying the approach of the occult and of secular psychology. If we allow ourselves and our understanding to become influenced and tainted by the false interpreters, it will only hinder our own maturity and accuracy levels when interpreting. Our understanding, at best, will become darkened understanding, twisted and unreliable. Their approach to interpreting is rather enticing because one may feel like there is power in it, but it is an ungodly power. The occult is not void of power, including the dream interpretation perspectives they are offering naïve searchers.

Tragically, many in the church today have turned to books and other tools on dreams and dream interpretation that are written by psychics, mediums, and other dark individuals. Such authors are influenced by some form of divination and the occult. This fact saddens me deeply. Over the past few years, many who have come to our dream interpretation outreaches in bookstores and other locations were in fact Christians looking for answers to their dreams. They had mistaken us as being involved in the New Age or the occult. This was partly because our approach was to go in "stealth" and not be quite as overt as other evangelistic strategies. Yet, these sincere believers were so desperate for understanding they would seek answers even in places they mistakenly thought were New Age. Many Christians simply have never associated dream interpretation with the church or the Kingdom of God and assumed we weren't Christians. They sought the counterfeit because they weren't finding in the church the understanding, power, or insight that they needed to understand the questions they were faced with in their spirituality and dream life. The result was that they went somewhere known to have answers to dreams in order to find some help or relief to their unrest and dilemma. This trend sends a powerful message that needs to be heard today by the leaders of the church.

> *My people are destroyed for lack of knowledge.*
>
> *Hosea 4:6a*

Let me say here that this is a part of my concern about some contemporary models of church. They fail to provide the spiritual meat that many are searching for today, and could potentially leave people worse off then when they came in to the Kingdom of God.

> *For it is impossible for those who were once enlightened, and have tasted of the heavenly gift, and were made partakers of the Holy Ghost and have tasted the good word of God, and the powers of the world to come, if they shall fall away, to*

renew them again unto repentance; seeing they crucify to themselves the Son of God afresh, and put him to an open shame to be burned.

Hebrews 6:4-7

The frustration of not knowing what a dream means will drive people to seek an answer. Nebuchadnezzar did this when he was troubled by his dreams.

And in the second year of the reign of Nebuchadnezzar, Nebuchadnezzar dreamed dreams, wherewith his spirit was troubled, and his sleep brake from him. Then the king commanded to call the magicians, and the astrologers, and the sorcerers, and the Chaldeans, for to shew the king his dreams. So they came and stood before the king. And the king said unto them, I have dreamed a dream, and my spirit was troubled to know the dream.

Daniel 2: 1-3

He first went to his Babylonian court of astrologers, magicians and Chaldean's to see if they could tell him his dream and the meaning of it. But even they couldn't help him, because the dream and its meaning were hidden from them. His dream was from God and they were not and therefore they could not answer the king.

If we allow this void in the 21st Century church to continue, thus failing to provide dreamers with answers that come from the God of Heaven to satisfy the quest of those who are dreaming, who knows where these people may find themselves. Remember, our adversary the devil prowls about seeking to devour whom he may *(2 Peter 6:8)*. Such is the ultimate demise of the sincere but misguided Christians searching for answers in potentially harmful places in spite of the clear warnings of scripture against such things.

Thank God many have been led to us in our public outreach dream interpretation events, but what about those who haven't found a pure source of light because the church has not been properly equipped, seasoned or matured in this arena? I don't say that to "blow our own horn", but rather because in their coming to us, they encountered the light and grace of God, and were spared the potential demonization resulting from exposure to the evil spirit and power of the occult.

Dreams and the Church

My goal is to see dream interpretation become a regular part of our training programs in every church and prophetic ministry across America and beyond, reaching to the nations. My prayer is that we as the church, by the power of the Spirit, would become attractive to the world, rather than the church desiring what the world has to offer. Too often we naively look for power in the world, but that power will only serve to destroy us. We cannot afford to ignore this issue of dreams and dream interpretation in this season of history, and in fact I believe the Lord won't allow us to. Therefore, our *paradigm* must radically change. We need to begin to have answers for those who are dreaming, even world political leaders to whom God is speaking. Through our God given interpretive skills & abilities we can provide the solution just as Daniel did to Nebuchadnezzar. A great opportunity is at hand that can be potentially revolutionary and change the course of history if we are faithful and wait on the Lord of Hosts. Scripture tells us in the book of Joel,

> *And it will come to pass afterward, that I will pour out my spirit upon all flesh; and your sons and your daughters shall prophesy,* ***your old men shall dream dreams****, your young men shall see visions.*
>
> *Joel 2:28*

This often-quoted text speaks of the dynamic work of God the Holy Spirit in the last days, in which we're privileged to be living now. Unfortunately, the church in this season and time has usually focused on other matters of less importance and has neglected or largely overlooked this significant topic of dreams, night visions, and dream interpretation. We live in a largely pragmatic western society with a scientific worldview that often doesn't make much room for things so subjective as dreams and night visions. Perhaps the reason we have neglected this area of study and discipline is because we have assumed God would raise up these types who interpret dreams if He wanted them. Have we assumed that this just isn't for the "larger" part of the body of Christ? Or has the reasoning been that if it is only for the more mature and therefore it is a more specialized type of ministry focus for a chosen and select few?

To the contrary, I argue that if we're all dreaming (because the Holy Spirit is being poured out as Joel prophesied), then we all can interpret. The wind blows where it pleases, and so it is with the Holy Spirit. The Spirit can move on us in any occasion, to manifest any gift He desires, according to His purpose in that given occasion. (*1 Corinthians 12:11*) The Spirit distributes various gifts as He wills. Joseph of the Old Testament so eloquently stated, "Do not interpretations belong to God?" (*Genesis 40:8*). Therefore, it is God who lives in us and who can give any of us an interpretation, or part of an interpretation, at any time. Just as all can prophesy, heal the sick, cast out demons, or receive words of knowledge by the Holy Spirit, so all can interpret dreams and night visions by the same Holy Spirit.

Theological Considerations

Some theologically struggle with the fact that a gift of interpreting dreams is not listed in the New Testament as are other categories of gifts, such as the lists mentioned in 1 Corinthians 12, Romans 12 and Ephesians 4. But because it is not listed as a New Testament gift, do we therefore fail to accept the reality of such a gift when it is obviously manifest in the Old Testament? Did God somchow change? Does He not provide what we need today? Have we ceased to dream? Have we ceased to receive dreams from God? Would He then provide a dream and not a gift or anointing to interpret it? No, it is completely contrary to God's character and divine nature to do so. What about other gifts and practices that aren't directly mentioned in the New Testament or part of these gift categories, yet the church embraces them such as worship leader, counselors, etc. Could this aspect and expression of the Spirit be inferred or implied in texts such as 1 Corinthians 13, which speaks of the gift of prophecy and knowing all mysteries?

There will be various levels of maturity and gifting among interpreters, just as there are various levels of maturity and gifting among apostles, prophets, pastors, teachers, evangelists, and those who are gifted in other ministries of the Spirit. Not all will be as Daniel, having understanding in *all* dreams and visions *(Daniel 2)*, but in our team oriented outreaches, and in our prophetic gatherings and communities, we can expect God to collectively give us understanding to the meaning of our dreams as we seek the answer from Him.

Though dreams, night visions, trances, visitations and other spiritual experiences are subjective in nature, God has chosen throughout history to speak to men and women through these means. Dreams and night visions have been among His chosen vehicles to reveal truth. Clearly scripture and recorded history demonstrate this reality.

Prevailing Worldviews

Science and its theories are largely based upon empirical evidence and upon observation and not upon that which is spiritual. However, scientific discoveries will never replace our need for the living God and His Word; rather, they should lead us to Him. I do not despise science. On the contrary, I esteem scientific discoveries and have benefited greatly from this field of exploration, as have so many in our society. My point is this: could it be that in some cases we in the body of Christ have subtly allowed this dominant scientific western mindset to become a worldview in us as Christians that displaces the truth of the supernatural? Remember that our paradigms and worldview influences what we consider valuable in life and in the Spirit. Many have agreed with secular society's worldview, rather than insisting upon the values and supernatural realities revealed in the Word of God. What the Word of God reveals is essential to our faith and an ever-growing relationship with the Eternal and living God.

My hope is to shed some light on issues like this, which erode our understanding of the value of dreams, night visions, and the ways of the Holy Spirit. We have an adversary that seeks to steal and counterfeit everything that the One True God does. Our adversary seeks to distort and to deceive. One aspect of this deception is centered on what we believe overall about our dreams. For example, as I previously mentioned in this view of dreams that is anti-supernatural, if I could use that term. I have borrowed the term from Jack Deere; he refers to an anti-supernatural hermeneutic that many evangelical scholars in so called "higher learning institutions" have embraced and espoused for decades, and which the church has leaned upon so heavily for truth and doctrinal orthodoxy. Their interpretive approach to scripture blinds them from seeing the full extent of the work of the Spirit in our day. Satan's deception or misunderstanding can also surround that which is within our dreams when we are seeking to know the meaning of what has been given to us by God or in a dream itself. We must, therefore, guard against both sides of the coin to find the pure and untainted word of God contained in these revelations of the night.

Equipping is crucial and probably the most important issue on both accounts of the reality of God speaking to us in dreams and the interpretive process that is rooted in intimacy with Him, if we are to avoid the mistakes and pitfalls of past generations.

Practically Speaking

Instead of upholding today's highly complex psychological dream interpretation methodologies, my purpose is to help others to hear the voice of God through dreams and night visions. Scripture clearly shows us that this was a commonly understood way that God spoke and revealed Himself to men and women of old *(Numb. 12:6)*. I want to see Christendom return to such an understanding. Furthermore, I want to make some effort to help change the current paradigm of this valuable area of giftedness which encourages the process of revelation and knowing God. God has offered this gift to enable us to hear His voice and to know Him more intimately. It brings Him glory to speak to us in dreams and night visions. As we are engaged in seeking Him to understand them, we learn to act upon them appropriately and with wisdom.

We can potentially miss many valuable insights, truth and timely revelation if we fail to recognize and pay close attention to the things God whispers to us in the night season.

Furthermore, we could potentially overlook or fail to recognize God's ways. Job said,

> *If I say, my bed will comfort me, my couch will ease my complaint, then You frighten me with dreams and terrify me with visions.*
>
> *Job 7: 13-14*

This was God's way of dealing with Job, and he testifies to the fact. I think it would do us good to take a fresh look at this reality. We must return to our understanding of the ways that God deals with humanity through dreams and night visions. Our fears too often govern and guide us more than does the Spirit of God, when it comes to this area of the Spirit. I have recognized this in my own life at times, and in the lives of the others I've interviewed about their dreams. I hope that some of these experiences I've had and realities I've discovered will help you gain greater confidence in what God is doing by His Spirit.

I will also deal with other practical issues. I want to help you in your dream life as you learn to interpret and apply what the Holy Spirit is saying through your dreams and night visions. This will include aspects such as dream recall (how to remember your dreams), dream journaling, and other such topics of interest to the dreamer.

I believe there are clearly principles of dream interpretation that we can look at and learn from in scripture. Knowing these principles will help us avoid drifting off into what can seem like a black hole of a confusion and oblivion. Seeking understanding in our dreams and night visions can sometimes be very difficult as we are learning. Rest assured. Though interpreting may be a struggle and confusing at times, with faith, patience and perseverance, interpretations and insights will begin to come. Daniel sought the *truth* of the meaning of his dream, and so it must be with us (*Daniel 7:16*). We must seek to know the *truth*, not another person's opinion or good ideas, or even fine sounding psychological arguments, but the *truth*. Let's follow the pattern that the prophet Daniel set before us. He was an anointed, devout, God-fearing, servant of God. His heart led him to trust in the God of Heaven, and he was greatly beloved as a result (*Daniel 9:23*).

Dreams really can be a lot of fun. Some contain feelings of extreme pleasure and are intensely enjoyable. Like a fingerprint or a human eye, each dream from God is completely unique. Each contains picture language that is as original and individual as each of us are. As we embark on this journey together, prepare your heart to hear the Father's voice and to receive his peace, creativity, and insight. Learn to wait on God as you listen and meditate on the messages of each night that He brings through a dream or night vision. No matter how obscure it may appear to you when you wake up, or how much ambiguity there may be in your understanding, you will learn to hold onto the dream. All of this will develop a deeper love and worship of the Almighty God. This love is a response and springs out of the revelation He gives of Himself and His ways that are much higher than ours. Listen to the words of the prophet Isaiah,

> *For my thoughts are not your thoughts, nor are your ways My ways, declares the Lord. For as the heavens are higher than the earth, so are My ways higher than your ways and My thoughts than your thoughts. For as the rain and the snow come down from heaven, and do not return there without watering the earth and making it bear and sprout, and furnishing seed to the sower and bread to the eater; so will my Word be which goes forth from my mouth; it will not return to me empty, without accomplishing what I desire, and without succeeding in the manner for which I sent it.*
>
> *Isaiah 55:8-11*

May the Father of Lights begin to instruct you in every aspect of dreams and night visions along with their interpretations as you embark upon this journey (*James 1:17*). Remember, every good and every perfect gift comes down from above.

Chapter 1

DREAM RECALL:

Remembering Your Dreams

Dreams can be fascinating but at times they are difficult to capture and remember. Upon waking, our first thoughts are often directed and intrigued to consider what we have dreamed during the night. Some people might remember their dreams, but feel pressured to attend to more important things than these seemingly random stories being played out in their sleep. How could they possibly have any meaning at all, some might ask?

Many dreams don't make sense to us, so we dismiss them and go about our morning routines, essentially aborting what the Holy Spirit was communicating to us. The dream can appear as a random story that strikes us, but without having an interpretive lens we can't seem to make any sense out of what we dreamt. It is not unusual within minutes of waking from sleep, to forget the dream we dreamed in the night or the early morning hours just prior to waking up. By the end of the day, we can only remember fragments or bits and pieces of the original dream. So the story goes. Does this sound vaguely familiar? Has this been your experience with your own dreams?

Because of other priorities and responsibilities, we in the western world typically become focused on the day ahead of us rather than taking a few minutes to respond to the dream we just had.

Many people that I dialog with ask me this question, "Why is it that I can't seem to remember my dreams?" They go on to tell me a familiar story I have often heard. They sensed or knew they were dreaming, but could not remember what it was they had dreamed about. This is frustrating and such a common occurrence that some would even begin to accept it as that which cannot be changed. In other words one might ask the question, "Do I really have the ability to change something like dream recall and begin to remember my dreams, and furthermore, do I want to?" If this is something you identify with and want to change, then pay close attention. I am going to address how to better remember your dreams and thereby increase your ability to hear God's voice at night in your dream life.

Obviously, God is the Creator and Sovereign of the Universe and we can't make Him give us a dream, but we can by faith respond to the dreams that He does give us. Ironically, you may find that this will result in an increase in the amount of dreams that you receive from God. It is a principle that we must learn. This principle of responding should also take into account we often have seasons of dreaming where the frequency of dreaming in our lives varies.

Passivity
Can I Really Change This?

The first issue that I want to address in relation to our dream recall is passivity. Many people accept too easily that because they can't seem to remember their dreams that there is nothing they can do about it. The truth is actually to the contrary. Perhaps we have never been taught that we can change this condition. If we really want to dream and remember our dreams, then we can if we so choose. It may take prayer and some work on our part, but we can change this. The first thing we must do is prayerfully make the decision that we want to remember our dreams. In fact, I challenge people to go to bed thinking about this very issue. Once they have made the decision that they want to remember their dreams, I will exhort them to meditate on this at night before they go to sleep. Tell yourself some form or variation of this statement; that you are going to remember your dreams and that you want to remember all that you dream each night. Say this over and over to yourself as you fall asleep. Watch and see what happens as you do this and note the change that takes place in your ability to recall the dreams of the night before. This is a simple exercise and easy to do. Over time, it will begin to influence your mind and spirit and therefore, your dream recall muscle will become active and enhanced.

Another reason we may not remember our dreams is that we have been taught directly or indirectly that our dreams just aren't that important. Have you ever heard the phrase, "Oh, it was just a dream". Case in point. It is widely accepted that dreams are just dreams and really have no bearing on "reality." Nothing could be further from the truth. This type of mindset is more akin to a cultural worldview in our western society. This isn't the only reason for our *absentmindedness* when it comes to our dreams. Other factors play into this issue as well. Relationship struggles, drugs, poor health, how we handle stress, spiritual warfare, and our current circumstances all can play into our inability to remember our dreams.

God Speaks in Dreams

For you to insist on remembering your dreams is in essence a way of saying to God that you value what He is saying to you no matter how or when He chooses to speak. Are you concerned about your dreams really being from God? It's a good thing to examine and question this. Not all dreams are from God; we will take a closer look at the source of dreams in a future chapter. Be that as it may, consider the statement (and principle revealed) that the Lord made known to Aaron and Miriam when they spoke against Moses.

> *And He said, hear now my words: if there be a prophet among you, I the Lord will make myself known unto him in a vision and will speak to him in a dream.*
>
> *Numbers 12:6*

Clearly stated, God speaks through the vision and through the dream. He spoke that way in the Old Testament to the prophets and He still speaks that way today to many. The Holy Spirit is a prophetic spirit and we are becoming a prophetic people. We can expect that God will speak to us today in the same way as His Spirit is being poured out all over the earth!

Ask God to speak to you in dreams and you can be assured that He will (*Mathew 7:7*). It is His pleasure to speak to you. I recall in my own journey having a tremendous hunger to hear the Lord's voice, early in my walk with Him. I would pray day after day that God would speak to me. Daily I was disappointed. The angel didn't visit me. I didn't hear the audible voice of God; He didn't take me up to His throne or transport me to another location or any of the other powerful and great ways that I was anticipating that He would talk to me. Finally, I realized that night after night I was having dreams and often multiple dreams in a given night. I soon discovered that God was speaking to me after all, but initially I had another expectation altogether. That is what led to my disappointment. It was exciting to discover His voice this way and yet it presented me with an altogether different challenge. How would I ever come to understand the meaning of the dreams I was dreaming?

Our part of this process is to respond when God does give us a dream. When we fail to respond appropriately, we may in fact miss what God wants to say through our dreams and night visions. We risk continuing to go about discontent, hungry, and dissatisfied in our spirit and in our relationship with God. Jesus said it like this, "Man shall not live by bread alone, but by every word that proceeds out of the mouth of God" (*Mathew 4:4*). The dreams that God gives us are a form of revelation and His word to us.

We in the church cannot continue to live without dreams and visions and without a genuine spirituality or we will become deeply unhappy and disappointed with Christianity as we know it. Often our flesh resists the effort it takes to become the spiritual household God has called us to be. We fear becoming fanatical. Sometimes we would just rather ignore an issue like dreams and dream interpretation than make the effort to understand what God has in mind for us. We must remember that we are strangers and aliens in this world, and that this world is not our home. We are called to a life in the Spirit (*Romans 8*) that is eternal in nature. Therefore we must have a completely different value system that embraces dreams and all things of the Spirit, regardless how much they might challenge our present mindset and our flesh. We can expect therefore that our dreams are intended and meant to change us and the way we think.

The Night Season: Sleep Preparation

Another principle I will often talk to people about who want to dream more and remember their dreams is to spend time before bed each night by reading scripture and praying. By this practice, our mind and spirit become cleansed, washed and prepared to hear the word of God being spoken to us in the night through a dream or a night vision or by some other supernatural encounter. It helps tremendously by releasing the peace of God in our spirit and in our heart.

I have observed that how I go to sleep at night is often how I wake up in the morning. Let me explain that statement. For example, if I were to let the sun go down on my anger, I will usually wake up in the morning in the same frame of mind. If I am at peace when I go to bed and experiencing some measure of intimacy with the Lord, unless there is some type of spiritual warfare at night, then I will wake up rested and at peace in the morning with my spirit directed toward God and listening to what he has been speaking to me in the night. I have learned that if I will focus on prayer and worship or the reading of scripture prior to going to sleep, then I will wake up in a God oriented frame of mind. Simply put, this is what I call sleep preparation. I will take time to make sure I have nothing against another person and as far is it is possible with me that I am at peace with others. Extending forgiveness where forgiveness is needed and praying for others where there are still relationship issues that need to be addressed. With minimal effort, we can enhance our ability to remember our dreams by preparing ourselves each and every night. In time, with practice and commitment this will become habitual. We must learn to sanctify the night and our hearts, keeping them holy before God.

I want to offer a practical suggestion about prayer. Throughout my walk with the Lord, He has instructed me to consider nothing in my life as "too small" a matter to bring to Him in prayer. By this, God has emphasized to me the idea that I should learn to bring *all* things to Him in prayer. Jesus taught the disciples this same concept,

> *Ask and is shall be given, seek and you will find; knock and it will be opened.*
>
> *Mathew 7:7*

With respect to dream recall, we often have issues that are hindering our ability to remember our dreams, and a primary way to address these issues is to ask the God of Heaven, through prayer, to help us. If we are to have maturity in our relationship with the Lord, we need to hear his voice for ourselves. We need to hear what He has to say regarding our lives and our circumstances. Whatever it is that we need to understand to get back on track in hearing God's voice in our dreams, He will bring it to light if we will but pray and ask His help. It is important to remember our dreams, which will often impact our personal destiny as well as the destiny of the lives of others around us. We must insist on remembering our dreams every morning and not allow any demonic or natural influences to steal or hinder this ability to capture the dream and its content as much as we are able.

Improving Memory

Memory is the final part of the equation in dream recall I want to address in this chapter. As a practical exercise, work on things that will strengthen your memory. For instance, spend time memorizing portions of scripture. As you do this, more and more you will see how your dream recall is also affected, simply because you are exercising your "memory muscle". It will get stronger and stronger, over time, as you are engaged in using it. Not only will your mind be renewed by focusing on scripture memorization, but soon it will become second nature to remember your dreams in detail as you wake up each morning, because you have worked to prepare yourself for each night's dream experience. Finally, after you have put into action these suggestions, don't be discouraged if you know you had a dream and can't remember it. One last consideration about the whole area of dream recall is how the Lord may give us a dream and seal it up inside of us. In other words, there may be times and reasons why the Lord has not allowed you to remember the dream. Consider what was spoken by Job in the wisdom literature in the Old Testament,

> *For God speaketh once, yea twice, yet man perceives it not. In a dream, in a vision of the night, when sleep falleth upon men, in slumberings upon the bed; then He openeth the ears of men, and sealeth their instruction, that He may withdraw man from his purpose, and hide pride from man.*
>
> *Job 33:14-17*

This text tells us that there may be a dream or night vision that the Lord would give to us and then seal His instruction so that it is hidden from us and we don't fully know it. He does this, as the text plainly tells us, in order to keep us from pride. The idea of a dream or night vision containing sealed instruction suggests that there will come a time where we need to have the seal broken and the instruction made known to us. David implied the Lord doing this in his life as well (*Psalm 16*). How this happens is up to God, according to His purpose, who is the one who is at work in our hearts at night.

For too long, the church has been without understanding of this reality of God's voice being made known in dreams and night visions. We have settled for second best and surrendered our birthright, as it were. We have surrendered having access to a facet of the power of the Almighty and of the God of Heaven who possesses all wisdom, understanding and knowledge. Much of this aspect of God can be imparted to us by revelation through our dreams and night visions, if we will only become as children and humble ourselves to listen to what our Heavenly Father is telling us in our dreams.

Chapter 2
CREATIVE JOURNALING:

Writing Your Dreams

When people talk to me about their dreams I hear one complaint more frequently than any other. Some tell me about their experience that goes something like this. They recently had a dream they knew was very important, but in the process of awakening and preparing for the day ahead, they had quickly forgotten what the dream was about. Here is another similar common experience: the person had a dream, and awoke out of sleep, remembering vividly. However, thinking it was such a powerful dream they would never forget it, the person goes back to sleep *without writing it down.* Upon awakening later, they sadly realized the dream was lost or at best, that they could recall only bits and pieces of it. How frustrating!

Dreams characteristically seem to fade rather quickly and can be erased from our minds within moments of awakening. Some dreams are even hard to describe and can be quite elusive at times making the task of clearly journaling them much more difficult. Because dreams are of this nature we must therefore recognize the importance and significance of journaling the night's dream activity as a habitual response to each new day. This can take some measure of discipline, as anyone who has worked at this will tell you. Often and tragically the experience of losing enough dreams is the hard teacher that prompts us to commit to this process of journaling. Deep sleep and the tiredness our bodies feel when we wake up will seek to dominate our response. This must be ruled by our spirit and by our understanding of how important it is to capture our dreams immediately with at least the main points and preferably with as much detail as possible before they fade from our memory.

Of course, not all dreams are this way. Some we retain in our memory for years and can recall them at any time. These would best be categorized as "night visions". Most dreams however are easily forgotten if we do not commit them to the journaling process. Therefore, if we are going to be intentional about and committed to our dream life, it is helpful to practice sleep preparation as I mentioned in the previous chapter. The aspect of sleep preparation I'm referring to here that I did not mention earlier is to go to bed prepared to dream by having some tools or a way of recording your dream by your bedside that is within reach when you wake up. The goal is to effectively capture as much detail, as many of the main points, and general impressions or feelings from the dream as we can upon awakening (*Daniel 7:1*).

I personally make journaling the dreams of the prior night my first priority upon waking each new day. I will sit down with pen and paper in hand, thinking through the dream or dreams that I had the night before. Sometimes we will begin to remember them immediately and at other times, as we start the morning work and routine, or in the midst of a conversation we can suddenly have the dream flood our memory. We soon learn that we must quickly commit it to paper or it will be lost. It is at this point that we are often faced with a very important choice. Will we pay attention to the dream coming to mind or will we discard it for something else that may seem more important or more urgent at the time? Much of the outcome of our choice has to do with the attitude and condition of our heart. Still a positive habitual response can be developed with practice.

Writing the content of some dreams can be a struggle in its own right. We often experience or observe such strange things in our dreams, things that we have never encountered before or have no previous frame of reference for. Sometimes we have a difficult time even describing these things, so it isn't surprising that accurately writing them can also prove to be challenging. We see things that we didn't even know existed (and they may or may not exist but at times may only be a symbol representing something else) or that stretch our normal thought process. We can see animals or places or any number of things that are hard to describe. We can encounter buildings and objects that are a part of the dream language, which is generally symbolic and simply not a part of our everyday lives or the normal grid of our minds and thought life. This can be an opportunity for a more creative aspect of journaling than writing words. In instances such as these it can be helpful to draw a picture of the symbol or certain aspect of the dream to help one remember what it was exactly that was experienced in the dream. I have done this on occasions where I felt like words were quite inadequate to capture all that I saw in a dream symbol or dream experience.

My objective here is to help you understand the importance of writing or recording your dreams for several reasons. One, which we've discussed, is that elusive quality many dreams have, in that they are seemingly wiped away from our conscious thoughts within moments of coming out of sleep. A second reason for writing down our dreams is to begin recalling details and working with the dream by praying and meditating on it. In many cases, we may not know the answer to a particular dream right away. If we have written the dream out and we have a record of it, we can come back to it again and again as the Holy Spirit prompts us to review a particular dream. This is part of the dynamic dream process, which we will discuss later.

Journaling: A Procedure

Let me describe how I go about my typical journaling process, by way of example. I usually have a procedure of two or three different writings of a given dream before I consider the process complete. I begin with handwriting the main parts of the dream as I wake up in order to ensure that I will not lose it before the dream fades from my memory. Next, I go back and add details or rewrite the entire dream. This may be after I have started my morning routine or when I find some quiet time to write, usually during a devotional period that I have set apart for each morning. Finally I type it into a word processor on my computer laptop and then print out the dream. This part of the process will often be at a time in the evening or when I am working on my dream journal throughout the week and may not necessarily be a daily discipline. This enables me to have a file of it on my computer and a hard copy when I file it into my dream journal or large three-ringed binder. When typing my dreams, I will leave enough room to make notes for interpretation, thoughts, application ideas or questions that may come to mind at the time. Throughout the dream journaling process, I pray through the dream and its symbolism, thinking about its meaning and seeking the Holy Spirit for possible applications to my life, including any personal responsibility actions that may be revealed or required by the dream.

This is the journaling process that I have found that works best for me. There is a rhythm to my journaling that is fluid and changing according to different seasons and various things going on in my life. I realize it may not work for someone else, but my hope is that it could at least help you get started in your own style of creative dream journaling. With experimentation, you will find what does and doesn't work for you. Much will depend upon your schedule and time limitations in the morning. Another factor that will affect your journaling will be your overall outlook on dreams. My outlook is that I have learned to take my dreams very seriously, and I'm willing to go through this process and spend the necessary amount of time, prayer and effort to find their meaning

I also catalog each dream, usually by its title, so that it won't be lost and so that it is easily accessible for future reference. This allows me to access it later as the Holy Spirit guides me to do so. Remember what Jesus told his disciples as He taught that this is one of the things that the Holy Spirit would do. He would bring all things to our remembrance that Jesus has spoken to us (*John 14:26*). If we haven't initially understood the dream there may be times that the Holy Spirit wants us to refer to it again to gain a greater understanding of a past dream and its symbolism. This happens to me quite often, sometimes referring to a dream that I had several days ago, or several years ago. There have even been occasions when I wasn't dreaming all that much. I came to learn that the reason for this lull in my dream life was a way of the Lord leading me to focus on and spend time with past dreams that I hadn't fully understood and yet were relevant to my present understanding and process. Therefore, to help me catalog a dream for my journal as I write it out I always give it a title and date the dream according to the time and day that I had the dream. Then I file it in my journal or three-ringed binder according to the title or some other significant detail or theme that appears in the dream. This helps as a reference point to remind me about the dream and its contents. It's important to realize that we will not always have an interpretation or full understanding of some dreams right away. That is not to say that God is not interested in giving us the understanding right away or that He is somehow unable.

But to have the expectation that we will always have the immediate answer to a dream can lead to a great deal of frustration and discouragement. We need to keep in mind that many dreams require us to search and investigate the meaning of the symbolism and the dream itself. In some cases, it can be years before we fully understand the meaning of a particular dream or night vision. The reason for this as we have noted, is that the interpretation belongs to God, and with many dreams He has designed them as such that we must diligently look for the meaning and the answer to the dream. He will give us the understanding when He desires, and never before. He is in control of this aspect of interpretation, not us! In a sense, it is a spiritual paradox. We must search and investigate, but the interpretation belongs to Him. Therefore, we need to keep each dream in an organized way so that we can access it when we need to review it or spend time with it as we are waiting on the Lord for the answers that we are seeking from Him.

For instance, I might go about my daily routine when a past dream or symbol and its meaning unexpectedly come to my mind. At that time, if I don't have a dream journaled it is often frustrating if I am unable to remember the full dream and all its details. I have often experienced the regret of not having such a dream at my fingertips. My search for the written copies of such dreams has led me to dig through heaps of paper and notebooks to find the dream I was looking for, and often I never find it. Of course, this is very discouraging, and a lesson to be learned. An organized system of journaling is essential and can be quite helpful; saving you a lot of time and disappointment in the long run.

There are many categories in which you may wish to list your dreams once you have a notebook that could be used exclusively for the purpose of journaling. You may wish to put them into categories according to month. Say, for instance, you had two or three dreams a night for several weeks. It would obviously be a great deal of work to understand and journal each of them, but to categorize them according to month would be of great assistance. Another help might be to journal the dreams by title and content. For example, dreams about your bicycle, car or house, etc. You might title a dream "My Green Chevy Blazer" and file it in the car or truck category. You may also choose to do this by the type of dream. For instance, if you have a dream that is clearly a prophetic dream, a healing dream, or a warning dream. You may further want to categorize them according to the people who appear in the dream, such as George W. Bush, or dreams with friends, famous actors or actresses in them or dreams with unknown people and then create a file for these types of dreams.

Journaling your dreams in this way can be surprisingly fun, and I recommend setting apart a time for working on your journal as part of your spiritual rhythm and lifestyle. During these times, I suggest reading through past dreams and weeding through any dreams that perhaps were dreams of the flesh rather than those that are obviously from the Holy Spirit. These could at least be relegated to a notebook of lesser interest where you may come back to them at a later date if need be. I hesitate to tell anyone to discard any dream, but I do recognize a greater and lesser personal interest and value according to the dreams that are from the Holy Spirit and those from the flesh or some other source. It is in this case that we must use discernment, which is an aspect of the spiritual package of growing in the overall understanding of our dreams.

Biblical Precedence for Journaling

To end this chapter, I want to remind you of a few of the scriptures that describe instances in which the Lord clearly spoke to the prophets and apostles and told them to write the things they saw and to keep them in a book. This happened on several occasions. The first example is the prophet Daniel. It reads,

> *In the first year of Belshazzar king of Babylon, Daniel had a dream and visions of his head upon his bed:* ***then he wrote the sum of all the matters.***
>
> *Daniel 7:1*

In this case we can see a clear example of the practice of Daniel to write his dreams out and journal them.

A second example I want to look at is the prophet Jeremiah.

> *Thus speaketh the Lord God of Israel, saying, Write thee a roll of book,* ***and write therein all the words that I have spoken unto thee*** *against the house of Israel, and against all the nations from the first day I spake unto thee, from the days of Josiah, even unto this day."*
>
> *Jeremiah 30:2*

It was obviously a significant task to write all that the Lord had spoken, but nonetheless an important thing to God for Jeremiah to do. Surely it is only conjecture to guess how many of those words that Jeremiah might have received from dreams and visions, but in any case, the principle is that a journaling process was in place to serve as an example for us today.

Habakkuk wrote,

> *And the Lord answered me and said,* ***Write the vision and make it plain upon tables,*** *that he may run that readeth it. For the vision is for the appointed time, but at the end it shall speak and not lie: though it tarry, wait for it; because it will surely come, it will not tarry.*
>
> *Habakkuk 2:2-3*

To write the dream or night vision will help us to not forget what the Lord has spoken to us. It will help us to wait for the fulfillment of His promise. This is a powerful tool of faith that not only helps us in the interpretive aspect of journaling, but also the building of our faith when we remind ourselves of what God has spoken to us in a dream or night vision.

Finally, in the book of Revelation, we read,

> *Saying I am Alpha and Omega, the first and the last: What thou seest, **write in a book**, and send it unto the seven churches which are in Asia*
>
> *Revelation 1:1*

Not only does writing a dream or night vision become a tool for us, but there are even times when you need to share it with others and therefore need an accurate account of it. Sometimes in the process of time, details can become obscured and mixed with other things in our memory. If we have written it out clearly we have that accurate and responsible record.

Journaling has many dimensions to it, from remembering His promises, to the help and aid in the process of interpreting, to the sharing of the revelation with others when the Lord is guiding us to do so. If you don't currently keep a journal, my hope is that after reading this you will begin to. If you have been skeptical about the usefulness of such a journal, maybe some of these points and ideas will cause you to rethink the significance of such a practice and lifestyle of working with your dreams.

Chapter 3

THE SOURCE OF DREAMS AND NIGHT VISIONS

Dreams and night visions are quite common these days, and are frequently discussed in some Christian circles. Particularly in Third Wave, Charismatic and Pentecostal churches, many expect God to use dreams to guide and direct decisions and daily affairs. Through dreams, God could be addressing our relationships, businesses, careers, or even the church. Many understand that the application of dreams is broad and would include any field or interest, from science to government and political leadership, to dreams that speak to a child. It is commonly understood that a dream could provide guidance, instruction or revelation on almost anything we're concerned with. Those with this understanding might even ask, "What would our spirituality be without dreams and visions in the church?"

For others in the evangelical world, questions linger in their minds. One extremely important question is, "Can we trust that our dreams are from God, or is there another source?" Some dreams are so frightening, strange or troubling that the dreamer may wonder if the dreams could be from evil spirits or some other unknown source. No sincere Christian wishes to be deceived into trusting dreams that are not from God and therefore be misled. Another cause for concern is that many individuals simply do not know or may have not been trained that God could speak to them in a dream. With these thoughts in mind, we'll begin this chapter with the obvious affirmation that God does still speak today. In fact, one of the often overlooked and yet powerful ways He is speaking to His Bride and to the pre-Christian is through dreams and night visions.

God does speak to us in dreams today as He did in times of old in the history of Israel. Hebrews 13:8 tells us that "Jesus Christ is the same yesterday, today and forever." We know from Numbers 12:6 that God loves to make Himself known to us by way of dreams and visions. Our Heavenly Father is not distant and unaware of our needs. Neither is He uninvolved in our daily lives. Rather, He is near. The "Accuser" would like to influence our view of the Godhead. Our enemy would like us to view the Father as one who can't be trusted, rather than as the one who brings us dreams and night visions and speaks intimately to His children through such means. Contrary to the enemy's lies, God is always listening to the prayer of His people, and He is always speaking to us.

> *Every good and perfect gift is from above, coming down from the Father of lights, with whom there is no variation or shifting shadow.*
>
> *James 1:17*

Often the things that concern us will concern Him, because we are His children. Very often, God will use a dream or a night vision to reveal the immediacy of his omnipresence and the reality of His omniscience in a particular situation. He is Holy and He knows all things. This reality is many times demonstrated in dreams and night visions by the Holy Spirit rather than just a theological tenant or creed that we intellectually believe.

If we are concerned about the counterfeit to this whole arena of the Spirit, including dreams, then rightly so. Even a superficial glance at our culture reveals the counterfeit's perversion of the very thing God is seeking to use in His church. For instance, there was a popular television series introduced called "Crossing Over" hosted by psychic medium John Edward. This show regularly features the supernatural, with a major emphasis on communicating with the dead. The secular media continues to spread their influence (psychics) in such nationally known murder crimes as the Shandra Levy case here in the United States and more recently a prime time show called "The Medium". This short account is just scratching the surface but it demonstrates in a small way how our culture in the western world is in a growing dimension searching for answers and hope even in the deception of a dark, flawed counterfeit, such as the Occult and the New Age. I am not suggesting that God wants us communicating with the dead in the church. We know from scripture that this is an abomination and illegal for God's people. Please hear me clearly that the source of the knowledge these psychics is not of God but is twisted and a perversion and counterfeit of the gift of word of knowledge that the Holy Spirit gives to the body of Christ (*1 Corinthians 12*). Furthermore, psychics and mediums who fill the bookstore shelves with books covering issues of dreams and visions, prophesy and the supernatural; these have become quite popular and are in vogue today. Let's take a look at what the sources of dreams really are and see what God has to say about them in His word.

Three Sources of Dreams

The three basic sources of our dreams and night visions are the Holy Spirit, the human soul, and Satan or evil spirits. We could also consider our bodies as being a potential fourth source of dreams at times. Many people ask me how to distinguish between dreams from God verses those that are not. My response is simple, yet profound. Let me explain. I can't imagine God giving us an easy formula or methodology other than to rely on Him through an intimate relationship for clear discernment by His Spirit as to knowing the source of dreams. If we are uncertain when we have a dream as to whether it is from God or not, we can simply pray and begin to seek the Lord. Some would look for identifiers such as color, since God is the Creator and author of light and therefore color. This is helpful and contains a thread of truth, but the satisfaction of a sure and right answer still boils down to our growing dependence upon the Holy Spirit and comes out of our relationship and intimacy with Him. We must recognize and know His voice for ourselves. When it comes to dreams, when we begin to make rules such as looking for identifiers to tell us the source of dreams, surely God will violate them at some point in time in order to draw us back to Himself in relationship. God is jealous for us as His people and will let nothing take His place in our hearts.

False Dreams

- *Do false dreams still exist today?*
- *What are false dreams and what is their source?*
- *How can we recognize a false dream or a dream from the flesh?*
- *When we hear a false dream, what are we to do about it?*

The book of Jeremiah warns us about things such as "false dreams". This is another type of dream that has its origin in the flesh and not in God's Spirit. Let's take a closer look at that passage of scripture from Jeremiah and see what it has to say.

> *For thus says the Lord of Hosts, the God of Israel, Do not let your prophets and your diviners, who are in your midst deceive you, nor listen to your dreams* ***which you cause to be dreamed****. For they prophesy falsely to you in my name: I have not sent them says the Lord.*
>
> *Jeremiah 29:8-9*

This is actually a letter being read that was written as Jeremiah prophesied and gave instruction to those in captivity in Babylon. Jeremiah was saying that it was the Lord who has caused Israel to be carried away into captivity in Babylon from Jerusalem. After seventy years He would bring them to return to their land. Others were prophesying to the contrary, causing captive Israel to trust in a lie. The emphasis in this scripture for our purposes here is upon the phrase, "the dreams you have caused to be dreamed." This is a type of false dream. In fact, I would further consider any dream that is not directly from God a potential false dream. There may be variations on the theme or differences between certain types of false dreams, but what it comes down to is the true dream verses the false dream. The true dream is obviously sent by God and leads to God and His glory, the false dream leads away from God and His will. These particular false dreams that Jeremiah is referring to originated out of their fleshly desire to return to the land of Israel prematurely, when in fact God would cause good to happen, but not for another seventy years would their desire to return to their land come about.

Let's look at another instance and what the Lord says about the false dream.

> *Behold, I am against them that prophesy* ***false dreams****, saith the Lord and do tell them, and cause my people to err by their lies, and their lightness; yet I*

sent them not, nor commanded them: therefore they shall not profit this people at all saith the Lord.

Jeremiah 23:32

This is telling us numerous things, but it points out that we need to use caution about dreams that we hear that do not have their source in God. John the apostle writes another similar warning,

> *Beloved, believe not every spirit, but try the spirits whether they are of God: because many false prophets are gone out into this world."*
>
> *1 John 4:1*

Hebraic View of Man

Another way of understanding dreams that some would label 'soul dreams' is to consider biblically how man is created. Man is created by God, a whole being with these primary aspects; the human body, the human soul and the human spirit. Our spirit and soul consists of the immaterial aspect of our makeup.

When we have a dream originating from the flesh the source of our dream stems from out of this aspect of our humanity. This can happen when our lives are governed by our flesh rather than by a life led by the Spirit (*Romans 8*). We may want something so badly that we begin to dream about it. This type of dream, though generally not desirable, can be useful and indicate to us that we need healing in a particular area. Our lives are to be governed by our spirit and this must be our understanding as we seek to take authority over the flesh by walking in the Spirit. That is not to say that our body is somehow bad as in dualism, but the human flesh left to rule and govern our lives is obviously fallen, corrupt and comes short of what God has intended.

God is Spirit and those who worship Him must worship Him in spirit and in truth. Once we are born again by the Holy Spirit we begin the process of growth and walking in the Spirit (*Romans 8*). The rest of our lives are characterized by life in the Spirit that manifests and demonstrates the fruits of the Spirit, the gifts of the Spirit and the Presence of God.

Our minds are to be renewed, submitted to the Spirit and its authority. Our decisions are to be submitted to the will of God, which our spirit is created to know and do, and is quite willing to do, by the way (*Mathew 26:41*). The same applies to our feelings. They are to be bearing the fruit of the rule of our spirit (*Galatians 5:22-23*). Remember what Jesus taught his disciples when He said, that which is born of the Spirit is spirit, and that which is born of the flesh is flesh. If we are born again, we are born of the Spirit and the new focus of our lives now and for eternity is spirit and not what is earthly and temporal, or born of the flesh. The flesh profits nothing, but the words of Jesus are spirit and life.

Personal Pilgrimage

Personally, I come from an evangelical background that has embraced the power, presence and work of the Holy Spirit. Even as early as my conversion to Christ, dreams and night visions have always played a significant role in my relationship with God. In fact, I do not ever recall dreaming prior to my conversion to Christ. During those formative years of my Christian walk, my experience with God was further reinforced as our church embraced and accepted that God healed and moved by His Spirit in many ways and dreams easily fit in our theology of the Kingdom of God, which had it's origins of the work of George Eldon Ladd.

It was during this season that I became more intimately involved in searching out the meaning of my own dreams and night visions. Hearing the dreams and visions of those in church leadership was instrumental in validating this dynamic and vital aspect of the voice of the Holy Spirit. But it was really icing on the cake, as God had already been at work preparing me from the beginning of my conversion.

To date, I have personally had thousands of dreams and have interpreted many of my own dreams and the dreams of others. I have much confidence that many of the dreams we receive come from God and not from the evil one. I suppose that comes out of my view of the Sovereignty of God. I trust that God will confirm those things He is saying to us through a dream or night vision. It is true that when one works with the genuine or "real thing" long enough, the counterfeit becomes obvious.

I have also had opportunities over the years to be in many other settings, such as Pentecostal, Charismatic and Third Wave churches in the United States and abroad. Many of these churches have seen and experienced how God is speaking to His church through dreams and night visions. Such churches and their leaders have begun to understand that if we want to hear the voice of God, we must come to embrace and listen to the dreams we dream. This excites me tremendously as I observe what the Holy Spirit is doing today. I see the potential fruit that can come from those who are serious and willing to pay the price to hear God by paying attention to their dreams. This is often a high price to pay, as it involves ambiguity, being misunderstood, being labeled, and can also include suffering on many levels. Consider for a moment the life of Joseph of the Old Testament and the misunderstanding he endured and suffered with his own family (*Genesis 40*). Those closest to him envied and hated him because of his dreams. That is not to say that we will all go through this. But Joseph is a model for us and we must recognize the different facets of his journey and process and how that same pattern might be worked out in our life in God.

It has become my conviction that in one-sense dreams and dream interpretation really isn't all that new. Furthermore, it isn't so much about where we go to church or about our eschatological views, as it is about God, who is Spirit. His voice and the language He speaks is Spirit. He has spoken in times of old through dreams and visions for his purposes in redemptive history. Today He continues the same activity with ever increasing measures of the outpouring of His Spirit (*Joel 2:28*).

In our zeal and immaturity, we often misunderstand and misinterpret our dreams and night visions and do things that immature people do in their spiritual lives. This is simply part of the process of learning to grow up in all things into Christ who is the Head of the Body (*Ephesians 5:23*). If we fail to understand that, we will look at some of the messes in our churches and become skeptical about dreams and the vital role they play in our maturation process. We can become critical and harden our hearts against the Spirit of God who is ever wooing and drawing us closer. We must make room in our churches for this growth process in order to have the greatest amount of fruit as it relates to dreams and dream interpretation. Babies do not immediately become adults, nor do immature dreamers become gifted interpreters such as Daniel or Joseph overnight. I see a revolution happening in the church that is restoring these valuable gifts of God and their operation in our midst. This awakening will benefit the body of Christ in preparation for the return of the Lord Jesus, but we must recognize the process that many are going through to reap the greatest harvest. May God receive all the glory and honor for what he does through prophesy and revelation, including dreams and night visions in these last days.

> *Beloved, I wish above all things that thou mayest prosper and be in health, even as thy soul prospereth.*
>
> *3 John 1:2*

The Value of Dreams

We live in a time of church history that could be characterized much like the Laodicean church and its condition that is spoken of in the book of Revelation (Revelation 3:17). We too are naked, blind, wretched and poor and yet we think we are rich and have need of nothing. This Laodicean mindset is the very thing that will hinder our pursuit of the humble (and sometimes simple) things of God, such as impressions, a dream or night vision. The church must come to a place where she recognizes the value of the things of the Spirit again including dreams and visions. We need spiritual eye salve to be put upon our eyes if we are truly going to see all God would have us to see about Himself in the Spirit. This includes being able to distinguish the fact that a dream is of eternal significance. We must realize that to fully hear the voice of God, we must begin to work with our dreams rather than just simply discard them as hardly relevant or "just a dream."

Another reason we may not understand the value of a dream and its significance is from a lack of training. By and large, we simply don't train people to listen to their dreams and work with them. Rather, in the church we often teach a person to be skeptical of anything that is experiential in nature, especially of anything that is subjective. An argument you might hear is, "That just isn't practical, nor is it really helping people to grow". This ought not to be. Just take a look at the many paradoxes in scripture to see what the nature of our God really is. We must change the current paradigm to embrace everything that God would say to us, and embrace every way He might choose to speak to us, whether it is through His still small voice, through a dream or through a visitation of an angel. He is God and we aren't. We must learn to follow Him and His ways, not our own. We must learn to separate what is our agenda from what is His agenda. Man's ways will always lead to a deep dissatisfaction, frustration and distrust. God's ways will bring life and freedom when we walk in them. For too long, the church has embraced a man-made religion. We must now, more than ever, be led by the Spirit. Obedience is an important key to unlock this type of lifestyle. For us to go where God has invited us, we will have to walk out and observe obedience to a much greater extent than we currently do!

A Radical Paradigm Shift

How do we change the current paradigm? What will that take? It begins with an individual and it begins with leaders. One of the greatest ways a mindset or paradigm can begin to change is to be impacted by teaching such as this book centered on hearing the voice of God. It can be through a closer study of dreams throughout church history. So little is written about what the early church Fathers said about dreams. I think if we knew what some of the dreamers who led the way in the early church said about dreams, that their influence would radically change the way we think about dreams today. It would change our understanding of God and His ways, and help create a dynamic and creative people that could revolutionize and bring reformation to the church.

Another way this mindset can be changed is by experiencing the power of God through a dream interpreted. This can literally change the dreamer's life. Unfortunately this hasn't happened very much in recent years. In the years to come as high level Christian interpreters are developed we will begin to see more of this. I have had such an experience and I have seen others have this experience. When they suddenly come to know the meaning of their dream, they burst into tears and are moved for hours and sometimes days, as they learn the meaning of a dream, which has often troubled them for years. This is the effect the Spirit of God has upon the human spirit. It is a powerful experience to become overcome by such awareness and understanding. The eternal, living God and the Creator of all things has a destiny and plan in store for each of those who love Him. He most often reveals His plan through some form of prophecy such as dreams or a night vision, just as He did with announcing the name of Jesus and the scandalous pregnancy of Mary in a dream. Revelation is powerful; that's why Satan and his demons hate it so much.

I have seen this kind of demonstration of the Spirit happen with people of many types, from the youth in dream interpretation outreaches to those of every color, nationality, language and ethnic group. Like the message of the Gospel of

Jesus Christ the barriers that typically separate people socially are transcended by the work and activity of the Holy Spirit.

The Ebb and Flow of Dream Interpretation

Like any ministry of the Spirit, there is an ebb and flow to dream interpretation that may be viewed as peaks and valleys. At its peak it is explosive. In the valley it is hard going, but just as important and valuable. Some of the ground can be quite hard, and like rough terrain to the beginner or novice interpreter. But the more one hears the voice of God through dreams and night visions, the more the treasure becomes a reality. I have witnessed this as we have interpreted dreams for the lost in bookstores, coffeehouses and on college campuses, and in what we could call Dream Labs or Dream Guilds. Many dreams seem to disturb us with what we consider strange content and are difficult to understand. But given time, reflection and meditation, many come to see that the symbols in their dreams really do have significance in their lives. This understanding can change and challenge how they perceive things spiritually and relationally.

In my opinion, we have missed out on so much in the church during these last days because we have chosen to ignore the warnings from God that could have saved us years of hardship. Can we afford to keep doing this? I think we need to ask ourselves some hard questions about what we really believe concerning the issue of dreams and night visions, and take a fresh look at how they can play a vital role in our churches today. Will we side with a Post-Modernist mindset of intellectualism, or with the cessationists who say that the gifts of the Spirit have ceased at the close of the apostolic age and the cannon of scripture? Will we continue to choose man's ways as opposed to God's ways (that may appear a little foolish to the naked eye)? Are we now trying to please men? I argue that we can't afford to and whatever it takes, we must return to listening to the voice of God through our dreams and visions and in any way He chooses to speak to us, so that we might more *fully* know Him and His ways. Remember the writer of the Proverbs, the core of Hebrew wisdom literature that tells us,

"There is a way that seems right unto man, but the way thereof leads to death." (*Proverbs 14:12*).

Chapter 4
THE LANGUAGE OF THE SPIRIT:
Dark Speech, Hard Sayings, Riddles, Parables, Metaphors and Symbols

The dreams and night visions that we receive from God contain the language of the Spirit and will challenge the way that we normally think, especially those of us raised and educated in western cultures like those of North America, Australia or the United Kingdom.

To fully understand the language of the Holy Spirit, we must examine parables and other expressions of divine speech more closely. Jesus said,

> *It is the Spirit who gives life; the flesh profits nothing, the words that I have spoken to you are spirit and life.*
>
> *John 6:63*

Jesus often spoke in parables and on at least one occasion we are told,

> *All these things spake Jesus unto the multitude in parables; and without a parable spake he not unto them, that it might be fulfilled which was spoken by the prophet, saying, I will open my mouth in parables; I will utter things*

which have been kept secret from the foundation of the world.

Mathew 13:34-35

As we have noted, Jesus spoke to his followers in parables and the meaning was often hidden from those to whom He spoke. This type of divine communication was in keeping with the tradition used by the prophets from ancient times. Jesus' use of parables then is a continuation of the long line of prophetic tradition in Israel. Though there are only seven such parables recorded in the Old Testament, Jesus takes this parabolic method to a whole new level. Jesus, the living Christ, is still doing the same today. Today, often these "parables" are expressed in revelation such as dreams and night visions in order to communicate divine truth.

Let's start by considering what a parable is by definition. *Parable* can be defined as, "To throw alongside, which implies that the literal details represent something else, and this is the essential method of symbolism." A parable, then, is a simple story that portrays everyday life, as the people of the times knew it. For example Jesus' parable about "the tares of the field" reflected the agricultural lifestyle of the times. Let's take a closer look at this parable.

The kingdom of heaven is likened unto a man which sowed good seed in his field: But while the man slept, his enemy came and sowed tares among the wheat, and went his way. But when the blade was sprung up, and brought forth fruit, then appeared the tares also. So the servants of the household came and said to him, sir, didst thou not sow good seed in thy field? From whence then hath it tares? He said unto them, an enemy has done this. The servants said unto him, Wilt thou then that we go and gather them up? But he said, Nay; lest while ye gather up the tares, ye root up also the wheat with them. Let both grow together until the harvest: and the time of the harvest I will say to the reapers, Gather ye together first the tares, and bind them in bundles to burn them: but gather the wheat into my barn.

Mathew 13:24-30

This parable when it was spoken contained symbolic language that reflected the lifestyle of the times. It was largely an agrarian culture within Israel, and this parable speaks in terms of the seed, the man who sowed the seed, the field, the enemy, the tares and the wheat. These all spoke to what was common to the people of the times, and they understood clearly what Jesus was speaking about when He told them this parable.

Today we also experience words from God in revelation, prophecy and dreams that reflect life, as we know it with all of our cultural understanding. Some scholars would call this *realism*. Often the situations they represent are utterly routine and the people are commonplace. Parables often portray social customs rooted in a particular time and place. Many times the actors in the parables are unknown to us as in Jesus' parables, rather they are types. Does this sound like any of the language you find in your dreams? Do you see people dressed in a style that you might see in everyday life? Do you see other things that are cultural signs such as cars, houses, and hairstyles to name a few examples?

The definition of the word "parable" tells us that there is some symbolic reference or an allegorical level of meaning to the story given. The word parable also means, "the technique of second meaning" implying a comparison between two things that are set alongside each other. The Dictionary of Jesus and the Gospels has some revealing insights about the nature and purpose of parables. The Greek word *parabole* has a much broader meaning in the Gospels than the English word parable. It can be used of a proverb, a riddle, a comparison, or a contrast in both simple and complex stories.

In Hebrew, the word used is *mashal. A mashal* is any dark saying intended to stimulate thought. In addition, it can be used of a taunt, a prophetic oracle, or a byword. There are also at least four different forms of parables. They are often distinguished similitude, example story, parable and allegory. Understanding parables can be helpful to see how the Lord would use dreams to speak to us in any of these forms for numerous reasons, even to stimulate thought.

Both the Old and New Testaments give examples of this type of prophetic, symbolic speech. When our dreams and night visions are from God they will also contain these characteristics. As we begin to recognize this language and see our dreams in this light, we will increasingly come to understand their intended meanings. God is Spirit and His speech is considerably different from ours. It too, is spirit, or a spiritual language. This challenges our linear thought patterns so common in the western world.

Take for example the dream and interpretation given to the Midianite soldiers that was overheard by Gideon and his servant Phurah (*Judges 7:9-15*). In this dream the Midianite soldier dreamed a cake of barley tumbled into the host of Midian and came unto a tent and struck it that fell, and overturned it, and that tent lay flat.

Can you see the symbolic language used in this dream? How odd this might have appeared to the dreamer when he awoke from the dream. When it was understood as it was interpreted, the meaning of the symbolism became clear to the dreamer, to Gideon and his servant as they heard it. The tent represented the army of the Midianites. The dream spoke of the victory of Gideon and his army. Let me say here parenthetically that this dream and its interpretation were given to heathen men; they were not worshipers of Yahweh. This is a point that we encounter in scripture again and again. We will come back to this concept in a later chapter.

Understanding Languages

Let's compare the concept of learning the language of the Spirit to the learning of a natural language. There are a number of parallels we could use to help us understand the process of growing as an interpreter of dreams. Such parallels can help us in unraveling the meaning of our dreams.

Some have a God given gift for understanding and learning languages. We could take that a step further and say that as interpreters of dreams and night visions we too, need a spiritual gift to understand the meaning of the language we encounter in our dreams. Even so, just as it is with most linguistic studies, grasping the entire language generally requires long hours and much work. The ability and willingness to make such an investment is part of nurturing the gift. So it can be with interpreting and grasping the Divine language of dreams and night visions that are from God. That is one of the reasons we encounter such difficulty with dream interpretation.

The gift is one aspect of the lifestyle of interpreting; the work of learning the language is another aspect we must keep in mind. If we take this analogy a step further, it could be said that just as most people learn certain elements of a foreign language but not all will go on to master it or specialize in it; they only desire to become functional in the language. So it is with dream interpretation. Many if not everyone can understand and learn basic interpretive principles. I think of it much like what the apostle Paul suggested about prophecy.

> *Pursue love, yet desire spiritual gifts, but especially that you may prophesy.*
>
> *Corinthians 14:1*

As the Spirit of God could grace anyone to prophesy, so all may interpret dreams and night visions on a given occasion if the Spirit wills to move upon them. "The dancing hand of God" is another way to think of how the Spirit moves upon whom He desires with His gifts. Not all are prophets, nor will all be called to the level of strength of Daniel in their prophetic or dream interpretive gift. More grace and light for interpreting may rest on one person than another. This reflects an individual's function, calling and purpose, not their value or status. We must therefore understand the gift of dream interpretation as a form of servanthood that carries with it responsibility before God in eternity. Let's look at some other scriptural references to the type of language God uses to speak to people.

Face To Face or Veiled Language

The Lord chided Miriam and Aaron when they had spoken against Moses because of the Cushite woman he had married. He said,

> *Hear now my words, if there be a prophet among you, I the Lord, make myself known to him in a* ***vision****. And I speak to him in a* ***dream****. Not so with my servant Moses; he is faithful in all my house. I speak with him face to face, even plainly, and not in* ***dark sayings****; and he sees the form of the Lord. Why were you not afraid to speak against my servant Moses?*
>
> *Numbers 12:8*

Here, the Lord reveals His divine order by setting a precedent and instructed Israel how a prophet could be identified; it was by dreams and visions. This was the speech of God, His voice, and His chosen way of communicating to His servants. The book of Hebrews tells us,

Jesus Christ is the same yesterday, today and forever.

Hebrews 13:8

He is still speaking this way today as He pours out His Spirit on all flesh! It is through the dream and the vision that God has spoken. It is through this "picture language" that God communicates to us.

Dark Speech

This passage also includes a reference to "dark sayings" which refers to the nature of the message in the dream or vision. Revelation contained "dark sayings" for most prophets, whereas Moses heard God differently. God spoke to Moses face to face, apparently because of his faithfulness, in "*all the Lord's house*" (*Hebrews 3:5*). So with the exception of Moses, every other prophet had to deal with dreams, visions and dark sayings. This was the Divine rule of the prophetic ministry in the time of the prophets of ancient Israel. Prophets had to discern the voice of God through the sometimes strange and seemingly bizarre workings of the Spirit in their dreams and visions.

What are "dark sayings" and why are they referenced in this passage? Why did God speak in dark sayings and instead of plainly, as He did with Moses? Does He mean to confuse us or even to hide things from us? If He is seeking to hide things from us, what then is God after?

Many questions begin to surface as we address the issue of "dark sayings" in dreams. But one thing we can assume is that our dreams will most certainly contain speech that is hard to understand. As with the previously mentioned parable, there will often be a deeper level meaning to a dream or night vision. Dreams are filled with symbolic references and speech that is "dark", which means that it contains hidden meaning. This type of speech requires us to dig deeper by seeking God to find the answer to what He is speaking in the dream. Remember what the book of Proverbs states,

> *It is the glory of God to conceal a thing: but the honor of kings is to search out a matter.*
>
> *Proverbs 25:2*

Many find that their dreams seem meaningless or strange or they don't seem to make sense at all, so they often end up discarding what is truly from God. We must understand that we are becoming kingly. This is part of the process of learning to understand the language of the Spirit in dreams as well as learning to identify which dreams are truly from God.

This side of God, or maybe we could say, this facet or mystical aspect of God we rarely talk about or give much attention to in the church. If we are really to know God, we must come to know Him in all His ways. It is ironic that as Evangelicals we believe in the authority of scripture but talk so little about these types of scriptural issues. I fear that in some ways we have "westernized" our view of God to fit the mold of who we think He should be, rather than knowing Him in all His attributes and in His majesty and splendor. We often entertain a different form of the Gospel to accommodate and please people as we tell them what they want to hear. To begin to explore this realm of hearing from God may frighten some; others may turn away from it as merely frivolous. Surely nothing will keep God from doing as He has promised He would do with the outpouring of His Spirit in the last days (*Acts 2:17*). We must begin to recognize that the author of inspired, inerrant and infallible scripture is speaking to us in dreams and night visions and His mode of speech is much like that of Holy Writ.

Let's look at some questions we have posed about this type of dark speech and begin to better understand the ways that God speaks. Our goal is to define a "dark saying" and thereby come to understand our dreams more fully.

David who was also considered a prophet (*Acts 2:30*) or the psalmist who writes Psalm 49, refers to dark speech. He says,

I will incline my ear to a proverb; I will disclose my dark saying on the harp.

Psalms 49:4

David of all men knew this side of God. The God of mystery who at times seems hidden, and whose creative speech was the parable and the riddle has a purpose in speaking in these ways and terms.

When Nathan came to David after he had committed adultery with Bathsheba, Nathan brought his word in parable. I'm sure you recall the story.

There were two men in the city, one rich and the other poor. The rich man had exceedingly many flocks and herds. But the poor man had nothing, except one little ewe lamb which he had bought and nourished; it grew up together with him and with his children. It ate his own food and drank from his own cup and lay in his bosom; it was like a daughter to him. And a traveler came to the rich man who refused to take from his own flock and from his own herd to prepare one for the wayfaring man who had come to him; but he took the poor man's lamb and prepared it for the man who had come to him.

Samuel 12:1b-4

This was a story speaking of an obvious injustice David had committed as he murdered Uriah the Hittite after committing adultery with Bathsheba. This was a prophetic parable that God used by speaking through the prophet Nathan. His speech was the parable and dark speech that required an interpretation that gave deeper meaning to the truth being revealed.

Many today, through intellectualism, have reduced God to mere theology. I'm not implying that the mind or theology is insignificant. However, in our over-familiarity, God has become someone we believe we can intellectually grasp. We have reduced Him and Holy Writ to our limited human intellect, which is nothing less than pride and a subtle form of idolatry. We must rediscover the awe of our Creator. The revelation in our dreams and night visions can help us to know Him better and inspire a righteous fear of the Lord.

Dreams and night visions can have that awe-inspiring affect. The patriarch Joseph said,

Do not interpretations belong to God?

Genesis 40: 8b

If we believe that interpretations come from God then we must come to deeply rely on and cultivate a dependence on the Holy Spirit for the answer to the enigma. He is the living God and we must know His voice and depend on Him for the understanding of His "dark sayings" that we encounter in our dreams and night visions. All of this ability to interpret accurately and understand our dreams boils down to a deeper intimacy and relationship with God. That is what He is seeking and I believe this is also what we are craving and longing for in this hour of history. Nothing but true intimacy, the Word *and the Spirit* will satisfy our hunger.

Dark speech is throughout the scripture. If we can begin to see with a new lens where and when the Lord spoke in this manner, we can absorb it, be transformed by it, and begin to learn how to deal with this type of language. It should no longer be unfamiliar to us, but rather something we regularly set our minds upon. Our goal ultimately should be to mature and grow in our understanding of how God is speaking to the church today.

For instance, consider Daniel and his interpretation of the writing that appeared on the wall. (*Daniel 5:5-9*) Though this is not a dream but rather a supernatural event, the writing was a "dark saying", or a hard sentence and required someone to interpret it. King Belshazzar saw the fingers of a man's hand appear and begin writing on the plaster of the wall in the palace, and his knees began to knock together. Great fear must have gripped this mighty Babylonian king as he observed this supernatural event and act of God occurring before his eyes. The king sought one to interpret the saying and none was found who could interpret among all the king's "wise men" of the Babylonian court. He was driven to find the meaning and understanding to what the writing meant.

I love what the queen says of Daniel as she suggests to King Belshazzar one who could interpret the writing,

> *Forasmuch as an excellent spirit, and knowledge, and understanding, interpreting of dreams, and showing of hard sentences, and dissolving of doubts, were found in the same Daniel whom the king named Belteshazzar; now let Daniel be called, and he will show the interpretation.*
>
> *Daniel 5:12*

MENE, MENE, TEKEL, UPHARSIN- Daniel interprets each word.

> ***MENE***- *God hath numbered thy kingdom and finished it.*
>
> ***TEKEL***-*Thou are weighed in the balance and found wanting.*
>
> ***PERES***-*Thy kingdom is divided and given to the Medes and Persians.*

Symbols and Metaphors

Daniel also experienced in his own dreams and visions the difficulties of the symbolic and metaphorical language. This happened to such a degree that the understanding of one of his encounters would only be revealed by the angel Gabriel. This example should caution and model for us to not rely on mere human methods alone for interpreting dreams and night visions. If we get caught in this type of mindset where we think we can know all the meanings of our dreams and spiritual experiences by simply knowing the meanings of symbols, we will certainly miss the mark and fall short of the truth of the meaning of the revelation. We must aim higher. The bottom line to this experience is that Daniel's ability to interpret did not come from his education, but rather this was the gift from the God of heaven who is Spirit. If God had not sent the angel Gabriel, Daniel would not have understood the revelation.

Where are the Daniel's and Joseph's for our generation and the next generation? We must intentionally begin to recover what has been long lost with the advent of the Enlightenment and other such periods of history that has robbed the church of the precious and valuable gifts of the Holy Spirit through philosophies such as Rationalism, Empiricism and Post Modernism. My hope is that with the reading of this book, you will take a fresh look at dreams, night visions and the supernatural. I hope you will see them in a new light and understand what they are showing you by the Holy Spirit. My hope is that these experiences will not be treated as something trivial and only of human origin or just a nuisance. We are a spiritual people and our God is Spirit. He is often speaking to us night after night, in times and ways we might least expect He would be speaking.

So What About My Dreams?

You might be saying to yourself, "That is all well and good for Jesus, the prophets, David and Daniel, but what about my dreams?" Dreams we have today often contain cultural elements that are relevant to our society and therefore to our lives. As with the language of the parable, your dreams and night visions will reflect common themes of the day and employ idioms that are common everyday life experiences. Dreams and night visions may also contain symbols and actions that seem quite strange to us. We just don't know how these things could exist, make any sense whatsoever, or *even be something to be interpreted.* For instance, what does it mean when a white rhinoceros is charging me in a field? I don't live in Africa so how am I to make sense of this? Or how do I understand driving a car with a full grown lion in the passenger's seat pawing my hand playfully while it is in his mouth. Or walking through a house in the early morning and seeing a full grown lioness and lion asleep on the floor in the house? What do I do with a huge 7-8 foot grizzly bear on its hind legs in front of me? How do I interpret swimming in a diving suit underwater? Or flying? What does it mean to fly in my dreams? So the question is this, how do I interpret those types of symbols in my dreams? Is this also considered another type of "dark saying"?

The answer is not easy. Sometimes it can take us years to develop a mature and accurate understanding of how to work with symbols such as these and others. We need to keep in mind that we are on a journey. This is a process that sometimes takes decades to fully mature. Wait a minute, did I say "decades"? Yes, in some cases I believe the journey is that long. But for some of you, it won't be that long. But for some it is a decade and possibly longer.

Something that might be helpful is to begin building files or a reference library, of these types of symbols that are of a contemporary nature, and seek the Lord for the understanding of each symbol and dream. In time, our understanding grows with the passing of each new symbol that we learn about in our vocabulary. This process should not discourage us, but only serve to help us grow closer to God and become more dependent on Him for the answers and understanding we seek. We learn these things like we learn the Word,

> *For precept must be upon precept, precept upon precept; line upon line, line upon line; here a little, and there a little.*
>
> *Isaiah 28:10*

The symbols mentioned above are examples of the type of language I am speaking of. They are God's spiritual picture language, which communicate more than words. This can be quite confusing at first but as we see these idioms used in scripture and come to know more fully the one who is speaking to us, then we will more easily grasp the meaning of what is being said in a dream or night vision. We understand how we are to respond and what we are to do in light of the dream and its meaning. This is called the application of the dream, which we discuss more in a later chapter

Chapter 5 MODELS *of Dream Interpretation*

The difficulty with dream interpretation for a Christian who is interested in growing in their anointing and skill to interpret dreams is that there are a number of sources that appear to offer help and insight for the would be interpreter. Unfortunately, most of these sources lead to the tree of the knowledge of good and evil. In other words, these sources are fleshly in their roots and lead to death. Remember in the Garden of Eden that God commanded Adam to not eat of this tree and its fruit.

> *Then the Lord God took the man and put him into the Garden of Eden to cultivate it and keep it. The Lord God commanded the man, saying From any tree of the garden you may eat freely; but from the tree of the knowledge of good and evil you shall not eat, for in that day that you eat from it you shall surely die.*
>
> *Genesis 2:15*

The violation of the command brought a curse. With this in mind, let's take a look at a few of these so called "sources" in order to identify where not to look for help in our growth process as interpreters.

Many individuals find a great interest in dreams as they innocently and compliantly take psychology classes in college. They become intrigued by the pioneering work and historical explorations of men like Sigmund Freud or Carl Jung, (who was a student of Freud's) Medard Boss, Erik Erikson and the like. Documentation of their experimental attempts to understand dreams as they relate to the human condition provoke and intrigue the serious student and the observer alike.

Likewise, college students often become intrigued as they learn from the ancient Greek philosophers and their approach and beliefs about dreams. Socrates, Plato and others have shaped many of the current mindsets and beliefs about dreams that we still embrace today in the educational system and in our culture.

Both the Greek philosophers and the modern psychologists have based their findings on the ideas of myth, folklore, scientific reasoning and trial and error. All of these are far from the source of truth in the Holy Spirit and the Tree of Life and can in no way be equated with His truth and revelation.

History and Cultures

The knowledge about dreams that comes from these sources can become quite confusing for a growing interpreter.

Indeed, some of the things history tells us about dreams are in fact fascinating. This leaves one questioning, "who or what is the final authority on this matter of dreams?" I believe part of the reason for this dilemma is that we are created by God with a void inside us. Even without Jesus Christ, humanity still remains fascinated by dreams. This broad human interest is clearly portrayed throughout the history of many cultures. From the Egyptian, Hebrew and Mesopotamian cultures to the Aboriginal, the ancient Chinese, and the Native American Indian. In nearly every historical and contemporary culture we find this intrigue and interest surrounding the power of a dream and its meaning. Even before encountering Christ, human beings will listen to their dreams and search ever so diligently to find their meaning. This is often done unknowingly in all the wrong places while looking to all the wrong sources.

As followers of Jesus Christ, how do we then guard ourselves from exposure to harmful and wrong sources of knowledge? How do we distinguish between the voice of God in a dream verses merely a dream of the flesh, or worst yet a dream from evil spirits? Furthermore how do we come to understand the meaning of a dream and the many symbols that we encounter in our dreams? Before we address these issues, let's first look at yet another flawed source of knowledge.

Another false or counterfeit source for the Christian interpreter and the final one I want to cover here before going on is one that is common and needs our attention. This source, probably the most harmful of all the sources, is the Occult. Even a casual glance at the bookstores reveals the interest in dreams that many people have today. Authors who often have an occult background or influence write incessantly on the topic of dreams, usually offering some new gimmick to invite the reader to taste of its contents or forbidden fruit. Such authors often present extensive symbol dictionaries that lure and deceive a dreamer and appeals to anyone searching for answers for the meaning of their dreams.

A warning to the wise is to stay away from these types of materials. It will ultimately pollute, confuse and darken your understanding. The source of these materials often is demons or evil spirits, and demons do not speak the truth. They lie, deceive and twist truth sometimes ever so subtly. Mediums and others who practice this form of divination or witchcraft write many of these materials and books. No matter how well meaning they may appear, it is a false or counterfeit source that will lead to destruction.

Not only is this true of bookstores, but also these same types of materials are prolific, flooding the Internet. There are literally tens of thousands of Internet sites of this nature, which have their source in the Occult. Some of this is presented in the guise of "God" language, as is common in many spirituality issues you find today. This of course is equally common in the New Age. To the discerning reader, *beware*. These materials may ultimately draw the unsuspecting, and in fact, they are so alluring and tempting because they have power. But obviously, it is not the power of God's light and mind in Jesus Christ. Instead, it is the power of the Evil One, the counterfeit, and is meant to destroy.

Remember, Satan doesn't care about you He wants to kill you! That may sound trite to some, but why do you think these books and materials are so prolific in the marketplace? They have a seductive power and they are meant ultimately to kill, steal and destroy.

Truth and Revelation

Where then do we turn? Where do we look for truth? Are there any models for true dream interpreters? Are there safe and reliable resources where a growing believer can turn? In this chapter, we are beginning to see that the counterfeit or false interpreters are available in several different forms. What about the real thing? What about that which is from God? Why don't we see more of this in the church?

Seminaries and bible colleges don't train or equip their students and future leaders to understand or interpret dreams. The church seems to have all but forgotten or misplaced this ancient gift of interpreting dreams and night visions. Could it be that Satan has sought to steal it from the church and the people of God? I think so. He has been somewhat successful up to now, but there are exceptions. The church is beginning to awaken and reclaim her full inheritance and that which truly belongs to her in Christ. I look forward to the day when we as Christians begin to flood the marketplace with dream interpretation websites, outreaches, books and other materials written on dreams that represent the true light and truth of our God spoken in a dream. I am jealous for this to happen, and part of the reason for this material. I hope and pray for the day when mainline denominational churches and seminaries begin to offer courses on dreams and dream interpretation. This should be a regular part of the training for those who are up and coming leaders and missionaries who have devoted significant parts of their lives to prepare for the service of God. This should be a part of the equipping process we all experience from the local church to every level of the leadership development process.

Chapter 6
MEDITATION:
A Tool for Understanding Dreams

One of the most helpful tools for a person who dreams is meditation. Meditation is a spiritual discipline and could be loosely defined as the art of concentration and focus on a given object or subject. For instance, a person can meditate on the works of God, the ways of God, the Word of God, the law of God, His testimonies, statutes, precepts and the name of God, to name a few (*Psalm 119:15, 27b, 48, 97, 99b, 148*).

All of these were given topics that enriched and deepened David's understanding of God, His ways, His creative power and divine nature.

Often, I will suggest to people that are stuck on understanding a specific dream or symbol to spend time utilizing the revelation in a time of daily meditation.

Unfortunately, the church often misunderstands meditation today. It is often associated with eastern culture and eastern religions. Because of our fear, we as Christians have missed out on a great deal of fruit, including spiritual insight and understanding that would come as a result of consistent and committed meditation. These are a few thoughts on meditation that often keep us from spending regular time in this spiritual discipline.

It is important for us to clearly recognize what keeps us from this time-tested practice. We need to identify the hindrance before we will be able to draw from this ancient well. It is a neglected part of our orthodoxy, of our heritage and spirituality, which is for every believer in Christ. Maturity in Christ can be determined in numerous ways, I suppose, but without a meditative practice our growth and to some extent the whole process of hearing the voice of God is affected.

My hope with this chapter is to introduce the reader to the concept of incorporating meditation as a lifestyle. I'll also give some guidelines that can be practiced in order to help understand a dream or a symbol in meditation. One of the most frustrating things I have found is to have a dream or night vision and not be able to interpret a symbol or a metaphor in the revelation. We must therefore devise ways to help break the ice or to change our thinking about the things we are seeing in our dreams or other nocturnal experiences.

Even as we read a particular passage in scripture it sometimes requires us to meditate to fully understand it, so it is with dream symbolism and the picture language of a dream or a night vision. To have a deeper understanding of anything in scripture, we need to spend time with it. We must allow it to get into our mind, our heart and our spirit before we can truly understand what is being said. Obviously, there can be exceptions to this, but as a rule, to have a fuller and deeper understanding of anything it could potentially take us years to know the truth in greater depth and breadth. Many of the riddles, dark sayings and hard sentences will require this of us, as well as other types of revelation. The goal in any dream or a night vision is to understand it as quickly as possible. But if we don't understand right away by the Holy Spirit, then it will most likely take place as a result of our search or investigation. The search can consist of this art and practice of meditation and contemplation.

Even Daniel asked Arioch the king's captain for time to seek the God of Heaven for the meaning of the dream that troubled Nebuchadnezzar (*Daniel 2:16*).

I can think of no better exercise than regular, consistent meditation to unlock the hidden meanings and dilemmas we face with our dreams or a night visions. As with any spiritual discipline, there are times of great light and fruitfulness, and other times when things are dark and often hard and laborious. Though we go through our devotions, for instance, we seem at times to find little value in what we are doing and it becomes a struggle that has either the potential to spiritually change us for the better or one that seems to defeat us, at least on an emotional level. So it is with meditation. If we recognize this dynamic, we can become stronger and push through barriers that seek to keep us from our goal of consistency and gaining greater understanding and a deeper spirituality.

Our seasons in the spiritual life of great difficulty can be just the thing that God is using to change our character, our paradigm, and teach us what we need to know. It is to help us become who He is making us to become. We must remain spiritually hungry and diligent if we are to truly find the answers to our questions.

How then can we begin this process? Here are a few practical guidelines to help get a person started. My meditation time always begins with a question of, *"What is it that is requiring my meditation time today (or this week)?"* I will take a particular dream or night vision that I know is from God, and read though it before my meditation session. I will find a comfortable spot that is quiet and where I will not be disturbed by phone calls and other distractions for the amount of time it takes me to meditate. I try to meditate for at least a twenty minute time period once a day. Obviously you can do this as much is needed or as much as you feel you have energy for. In the Psalms, David spoke of meditating both day and night (*Psalm 1:2*). For me, twice a day for meditation is not a stretch at all. I will usually focus on a given aspect of the dream or vision that has been particularly difficult for me to understand. Remember, it was said of Daniel that no dream troubled him. The approach I take is to have the same resolve and let nothing I see in a dream be something I can't interpret. I will persist until the Lord gives me the understanding. I have no trouble believing that He will do just that, because my confidence is in Him and not misplaced in man or a methodology. I will ruminate on each issue that troubles me. To ruminate means, according to Webster's, "To muse upon, to chew upon the cud." That sounds a bit funny, but the idea is that with a given theme or topic, one goes over it in the mind and heart repeatedly, often casually or slowly, and it can be for long periods of time. It can also mean to engage in contemplation.

Personal Example: New Discoveries

I will often tell the following story when I travel and teach on dreams and night visions because it impacted me so powerfully on this topic of meditation and revelation. This issue is born out of my own experience and my quest to find an answer to a dream I was certain was from God. Often, when I don't understand a dream right away my practice has been to pray through the dream and then sit on it and wait on God to show me things in the course of time in my walk and relationship with Him. Sometimes in that process, He will remind me of a given dream that I haven't fully understood. I will begin to intentionally spend time with it again by meditating upon it and reading through my dream journal.

On this particular occasion, a dream I felt was very significant came to my mind and not without coincidence, because I was reminded of this dream after two years nearly to the day of the original dream. I went over the dream again from my journal to remind myself of the details and decided to spend some time with it in my meditation session that day. Often it takes me time to wind down and relax my body, clear my thoughts of all distractions, worries and negative emotions. As I did this, I began to ruminate upon a phrase that was spoken within the dream by the main character that was a national spiritual leader at that time. He said to me in this dream; "*Don't you hate people who aren't in clicks?*" Truly a strange sentence indeed; this statement, from the time I had the dream, troubled me. It didn't seem to make any sense to me. In retrospect I seem to have had many dreams over the years with these types of fragmented and seemingly out of place sentences in them.

As I set my mind upon the dream and began to think on this sentence I realized suddenly what the phrase meant. I just knew. God graciously dropped the meaning in my spirit and I knew in the midst of my meditation time what this hidden and sealed revelation had meant. That was the whole point, I think. God was demonstrating to me and teaching me what Joseph said; *"Don't interpretations belong to God?"(Genesis 40:8).* Up to that point in time the dream was not interpreted because God did not give the interpretation. He is Sovereign and He will do what He wants, when He wants, and how He wants. In this case he decided at this point in time to release a tiny sliver of His mind and omniscience to me on the dream and its meaning. In fact, He seemed a little anxious to do so.

I suddenly came to understand that this portion of the dream when I was questioned, *"Don't you hate those who aren't in cliques? "* meant that I was being tested and the test had to do with how I would respond to this question. I said in the dream, *"No, I have compassion for them"*, then an ensuing encounter or empowerment of the fire and power of the Holy Spirit came upon me, which was forever engraved or etched upon my mind and my spirit.

What I came to understand about the phrase in the dream and how it was to be interpreted was that this was speaking about the outcasts of our culture, our churches, our society and humanity. If you think of the phrase this way, those people who are "in" cliques are those who "belong" to or are a part of a given group. Those people who "aren't" in cliques then are the opposite, or outcasts. I seem to have passed the test in the dream when I responded to the question right away and a new level of the Spirit came as I mentioned above. "Compassion" was the right answer and power followed after my response. When this understanding came to me I was overjoyed and in my spirit I was exuberant, to say the least. I knew that I knew, that I knew that this was the meaning to this little phrase within the dream. The ironic part was that it took two years to simply understand that phrase. I thought to myself that if it took two years to understand that one short phrase, what about the rest of the dream? This was a life-changing encounter with God that I will never forget.

God's ways and thoughts are higher than ours (*Isaiah 55:9*). I began to see two things in particular from this valuable lesson. One was that God graciously gave the meaning of the phrase and He did it in His time frame. The second was that He gave me the understanding in my meditation experience of all places and taught me the significance of this activity in relation to interpreting dreams and visions.

Since that time I have tried to keep a regular and daily schedule of meditation if for no other reason than for the dreams and visions that I receive nightly. Many dreams won't require me to spend much time in meditation. There are exceptions and they will contain things that transcend the mind and are spirit. In order for me to know their meaning to the fullest extent I have to meditate on them and the context in which they come.

Following is a list of Scriptures on meditation*:*

Genesis 24:63

Joshua 1:8

Psalm 1:2

Psalm 5:1

Psalm 19:14

Psalm 49:3

Psalm 63:6

Psalm 77:12

Psalm 104:34

Psalm 119:15,48,78

Psalm 119:97,99,148

Psalm 143:5

1 Timothy 4:15

Chapter 7
THE DREAM THAT CHANGED HISTORY

The story of the birth of Jesus Christ and the events that unfolded before His birth invite us to understand more about the significance of dreams and the important role they have played throughout redemptive history. God has always spoken to His people through dreams and night visions, and this occasion was no exception. We see the incredible wisdom of the Creator to use a dream in the lives of human beings. The dream not only saved the life of the Savior in His infancy, but also ensured His parents relationship from being irreparably damaged. There was a supernatural intervention in the dream to give divine guidance and understanding of the circumstances.

At pivotal times, dreams like the one given to Joseph of the New Testament are introduced into the lives of those whom God had chosen to speak. If we are to know the ways of God and how He speaks today, then we must come to accept the reality that God has entrusted imperfect, weak, and often broken human vessels with dreams to accomplish the divine will.

It is amazing to see this principle of the Spirit in action, especially in the situation with Joseph and Mary. As the story unfolds, we are told that they are engaged and are preparing for their marriage. Joseph discovers that Mary is pregnant and he knows full well that he is not the father of the child. Can you imagine how he must have initially responded to the news of

Mary's pregnancy? Mary, a virgin, is now mysteriously pregnant. Imagine how Joseph must have wrestled in his own heart on how to handle the situation. How would He deal with the fact that Mary must have been unfaithful to him? I can almost hear his thoughts, "Devout Jewish men and women don't live this way. What happened to us? What will everyone say? How do we explain what has happened? It must look as if we slept together before our nuptials and violated this holy and sacred bond. What a disgrace we must appear to be before our family.

Scripture goes on to tell us of the type of man Joseph was, that he opted to not publicly disgrace Mary, but thought to put her away or divorce her privately without bringing shame and further embarrassment to her because of her apparent unfaithfulness (*Mathew 1:19*). What a story. The plot thickens as we continue. It would be difficult for Mary to convince Joseph of what she had experienced. The circumstances would indicate her unfaithfulness and intimate sexual relations out of wedlock. "How could a woman become pregnant by the Holy Spirit" Joseph might have asked. A woman gets pregnant one way, and one way only, his rational mind might have argued.

This situation could not have been easy for either Joseph or Mary. How would she tell her parents and friends this outlandish story? What about the future prospect of her life apart from the man she loved? What would she do now? She must have been a little fearful about how he would have reacted to her news about the pregnancy.

Mary, a young Jewish woman and lover of the God of Israel, now finds herself in this place of controversy. She had found great favor with God and had been overshadowed by the Holy Spirit and was now pregnant. This was the plan of God Almighty all along. The Ancient of Days had known from the beginning who He would choose at the appointed time to give birth to the Messiah, the Son of David. This was the fulfillment of prophecy spoken by the prophet Isaiah.

> *Therefore, the Lord Himself shall give a sign; behold a virgin shall conceive, and bear a son, and you shall call His name Immanuel.*
>
> *Isaiah 7:14*

Somehow Mary now had to explain this to her husband-to-be. As it turns out, we again see a divine intervention that preserves their relationship. Yes, that's right; this dream might have saved their marriage and preserved the child's family.

If God saved this marriage through a dream, do you think He is beyond that today? You and I may speculate that this dream was only given because it had to do with the Son of God, to ensure the divine purpose of His life. But I believe that though it was regarding the Son of God, it is also an example for us to consider in a new light. Imagine how this might have application for us today. Perhaps we should consider all the misunderstanding that could be avoided or cleared up, if we simply listened to our dreams and understood what the Lord was showing us during crucial periods in our lives and relationships. I'm not suggesting this as an easy way out of relational conflict or communication issues. Rather, I am suggesting that there may be times when a dream or night vision may come and help us to see things from Heaven's perspective rather than from the perspective of our circumstances or emotions. Circumstances don't always tell the full story, would you not agree? Often, we need more insight or as in the case of a dream, we need revelation, before our hearts are changed and we are able to fully engage in the relationship once again.

Let's consider Joseph and Mary again. How did the God of Israel save this marriage? The scripture tells us that Joseph, as he thought on these things, had a dream.

> *But while he thought on these things, behold, the angel of the Lord appeared unto him in a dream, saying, Joseph, thou son of David, fear not to take unto thee Mary thy wife: for that which is conceived in her is of the Holy Ghost.*
>
> *Mathew 1:20*

In the dream, an angel of the Lord appeared to Joseph and spoke to him about his future wife, and about the child. As the dream continued, the angel revealed much more. This dream/revelation and its message not only enabled Joseph to understand his wife-to-be and be reconciled to her, more importantly, it also prophesied of the future of this child. This child was to be the greatest Hebrew child of all time and who would save His people from their sins. Additionally, the dream revealed the Name above every Name, which was to be given to the child. This is the first place we hear the name of the Messiah. The angel told Joseph what the name of the child should be. Interestingly, it was the father that the name was given to. Furthermore, it came by revelation through a dream, not by human origin or will.

What is in a name, you might ask? Well, in this case and in others in Scripture, great importance is attached to names. A person's name speaks of his or her character. In fact, a person's name often defines and influences his or her destiny. The child's Name was so important to God Almighty that He announced it in a dream and sent an angel to appear in the dream to announce the Name. This child was no accident, nor was His Name. He was chosen by the Father to be born at the appointed time to bear this name to accomplish the divine will of God in His generation which ultimately has reached every generation since, for over two thousand years.

How do you name your children? Did you know that your destiny and the destiny of your child could be revealed in a dream? Furthermore, how do you deal with relational misunderstandings with your spouse? This dream given to Joseph seems to imply that God is very interested in our relationships and He will even help us in this regard. As we seek to live by the Spirit, let's not limit God as to what He may do or say to us in a dream or night vision. Let's consider how our experience in a dream might forever change us, as He chooses to help us in a time of trouble or distress.

Revelation. That's what it took for Joseph to understand Mary and what happened to her. It took revelation for him to know that this child and their marriage would be different from others. The revelation further explained that Joseph had been given the responsibility to care for the child and raise Him in a godly Jewish family and heritage. The revelation in the dream empowered Joseph and provided much needed direction. I'm sure that until the dream came, this was a very confusing and fearful time in Joseph's life.

What if the dream had not come? What if Joseph decided to leave Mary and marry another woman? Could Jesus have been raised without Joseph? Probably so, but it wasn't God's ultimate intention for Jesus to be raised outside of Joseph's family. Furthermore, have you encountered fatherlessness in others or have you yourself been raised fatherless? Have you seen the devastation and the scars it leaves on children from broken families? Jesus would not have had the best father in Israel that he could have, nor the father that God Almighty had chosen for Him, had the dream not come to Joseph. This was not a flippant or incidental choice on the part of the Creator. Joseph, as the angel said, was a "Son of David" (*Mathew 1:20*). His blood was of pure Jewish lineage and the blood of the tribe of Judah, descendant from David. He had preserved the lineage of the promise of the seed of Abraham, Isaac and Jacob. This was no mistake. Jesus was to be born into this family and the dream ensured it and it would happen as God had planned.

The divine purpose and order was tied up in a dream. It is hard to believe isn't it? A dream had all this influence and power in Joseph's life. What if Joseph was just emotional and imagined all this? Can you hear the modern day arguments of how this dream didn't play the role it did in this situation? This dream changed history forever.

Another point of consideration is symbolism. Popular opinion is that dreams are largely symbolic, and many times they are, but this dream was about as literal as they come. There was no interpretation required. What it said is what it meant. Beware against interpreting when no interpretation is needed. This is not the only occasion in Scripture where we encounter this type of dream, which further gives support to the idea that dreams are not always symbolic. In fact, I know others today who dream very much like this. There are no easy formulas or methods in this vast subject of dreams, night visions and dream interpretation. We must simply and totally rely on the voice of God to show us the meaning and application of each and every piece of revelation He gives us. These kinds of dreams that are more literal in nature may by some be considered visions. But we cannot elude the scriptural evidence that this dream Joseph received was literal? There obviously are exceptions to all our "rules" and boxed in ways of thinking.

Angels in Our Dreams

Another consideration in this type of dream is the issue of the visitation of an angel. Joseph received a visitation from an angel in the dream. That means that the angel literally was in his dream and literally spoke to him in the dream. As we begin to look at this dream more closely, we need to ask, "Why did the angel come and speak to Joseph? Why did God communicate through an angelic visitation? Why didn't God use an appearance of Himself of some sort, or even His own audible voice? For heaven's sake, this is the Son of God we are talking about here! Why did God send a subjective experience like a dream and furthermore, why a visitation of an angel in a dream?"

As I have mentioned from the outset, Joseph's dream can be seen as a pattern for us today. It sets a clear example of how we, too, might receive these types of dreams and encounters, including visitations from angels. There are various other types of visitations we might consider here, but first I want to share a dream from my own experience.

Personal Encounters

Let me provide a little background information. I have often encountered angels in my dreams. They appear in different forms: sometimes they are silent, and sometimes they speak. Sometimes the angels are large and sometimes they are small. Sometimes they come in the form of human beings, sometimes they don't.

Many people are intrigued by what angels look like. People ponder if angels can come in a form other than what we typically think or conceive in our minds of what an angel looks like. Scripture reveals that angels can appear in different ways and forms. For example, consider the two men that came to Lot in Sodom and Gomorrah (*Genesis 19:1-3, 11*). In this case the angels appeared as two men. Lot first meets them in the city gates where he offers them lodging for the night. He later washes their feet and prepares a feast where they can eat together.

Furthermore, they display supernatural power as they struck with blindness those who were trying to get into Lot's house. All this took place during the angel's visit to Sodom and Gomorrah prior to its judgment. Also consider the three men that visited Abraham and Sarah and announced the child Isaac that was to be born in their old age (*Genesis 18:1-15*). The mighty and other various angels spoken of in the book of Revelation are examples, and so on (*Revelation 10:1*). These examples all help us understand that angels appear in different ways and forms;

some angels flying in Heaven, some here on earth appearing as human beings and more. Let me continue with an example from my own life.

I had a dream that I was driving my 1996 Chevy S10 Blazer. For some time, I was driving with a friend in the passenger seat, trying again and again to get out of a wooded area. The scene changed and now the odd thing was that I was driving the truck on top of water. It was like on a lake or some other body of water on a clear, beautiful day with sunshine and blue sky. My driver's side window was down and I looked into the water and there was a small girl in a white dress. She was beneath the surface of the water, yet she was looking at me from within the water. She couldn't have been more than two feet high; she was quite small. I couldn't see her face very well because the ripples from the water obscured a clear view of her face. Though I couldn't make out her face, I know this part of the dream was intentional and from the Lord. In fact, many times the people we encounter in our dreams, when we can't remember their faces, represent angels. In my dream, this was the case and was part of the meaning of the dream. I was not supposed to see the face of the angel, or I was not permitted to see her face clearly. As I was trying to get a closer look at the angel, she spoke to me. I could hear her voice, though she was underwater and I was above water and in my truck. She spoke only one sentence to me. She said, "I could have revealed myself to…(a particular church that I won't name here), but I chose not to." The dream ended.

This dream taught me a number of things. First it taught me that angels could appear in dreams as children. This small girl in the white dress who spoke to me from within the water was an angel. Why would an angel appear as a child, you might ask? One reason may be that she reflected the maturity level of the church this angel had been sent to. Another possibility is that doing so portrayed some child-like characteristic, such as innocence and purity. This dream also taught me that the angel had a will. Just as humans have been created with a will, we have freedom and must choose things, so also angels have been created in a like manner. Each angel has been given a will. The book of Jude gives us a glimpse into this truth.

> *And the angels which kept not their first estate, but left their own habitation, he hath reserved in everlasting chains under darkness unto the judgment of the great day.*
>
> *Jude 6*

Furthermore, what the angel said to me was packed with understanding and very revealing. The angel I had seen in this dream could have shown itself to that particular church but chose not to. What an astounding statement that seemed to me. Maybe this church wasn't ready, or maybe they didn't want her around? I can only speculate why the angel had ultimately chosen not to show herself, since she did not tell me why.

Though she did not explain her reasons, I could hear the sorrow in her voice.

Let me say here that because of what I felt in the voice of this angel as she spoke to me, I have become concerned that we can become consumed with our own personal and church agendas. If we allow this to happen, we can over the course of time, become calloused and hardened to the point of losing sensitivity to what is happening in the Spirit. We must return to the deeper place of prayer and listening to the voice of God. That only happens by spending time with God. We must become a people who are deeply committed to spending time alone with God and cultivating intimacy with the Holy Spirit. God's ways and thoughts are not like ours, His are much higher. (*Isaiah 55:8-9*). No matter how well trained theologically we think we are, if we fail to live in the way that God prescribes, we can potentially lose His presence and the full blessing He intends for us. This is at least part of the message that was being communicated to me in the dream. As we can grieve the Holy Spirit at times, (*Ephesians 4:30*), so we can grieve those He sends to us, as this heavenly messenger was sent with a particular divine purpose to a given church. This dream revealed the angel in the water, and in this case the water speaks of the Spirit. I was looking into the Spirit when I saw this angel and she spoke to me her message. In essence the dream was saying that from within the Spirit, this angel was speaking to me and revealing her choice and sorrow as it related to this particular church.

Angels play an important role in our lives and in our dreams as Christians. Joseph's dream contained an angel and so do many other dreams that the God of Heaven gives to us today. When the angels appear in scripture, it is to emphasize that the message about to be shared is a message of great importance and should not be taken lightly. This dream that Joseph experienced, helped him to overcome his fear as the angel spoke to him,

> *Fear not to take unto thee Mary to be thy wife: For that which conceived in her is of the Holy Ghost and she shall bring forth a son, and thou shalt call His name Jesus, for He shall save His people from their sins.*
>
> *Mathew 1:20-21*

Chapter 8
LUCID DREAMING
and Christianity

In this chapter, we will explore the topic of lucid dreaming. Lucid dreaming is a concept that describes a certain amount of control that we can exercise within our dreams while we are dreaming. This concept should become normative for our lives and experience as "Spirit empowered" followers of Jesus Christ. If it isn't already, my desire is to introduce and stretch the reader's paradigm with respect to this topic. Though for some this will obviously be a controversial topic, others will find that they really are having lucid dreams from God. Some of you may have already discovered that you are able to exercise some control within your dreams, and to others the concept may be a fairly new and exciting aspect of your journey.

One small indicator of a lucid dream that a person may experience is that they are aware that they are awake or conscious (or apparently awake) in the dream that they are dreaming. This can happen in numerous ways within the dream. Sometimes small insights occur that tip us off when we are first beginning to experience lucid dreams. As we become more sensitive to the ways this is happening, we can work with the dream while in the dream as we practice and respond accordingly.

It seems that the enemy has blinded the church to this facet of dreaming, and little has been written on the topic from a

Christ-centered perspective, to redeem what truly belongs to the people of God. "Control" is such a spiritually deadly term, and I hesitate to use it here. There are exceptions though, as we know from reference in the scripture to self-control, which is a fruit of the Spirit (*Galatians 5:19*). Abuses come when we try to control others, either knowingly or unintentionally. This is obviously not what I am referring to when I use the term control. I will attempt to explain this further as we continue.

Part of the reason I want to explore lucid dreaming in this book is to help bring clarity to the issue. I want to begin the process of removing any cloud of unknowing or ignorance that keeps us as Christians from entering into that which has been made available to us in the Kingdom of God. In other words, it has been my observation that we seldom investigate into this area of spirituality, primarily out of fear. I hope to help remove the fear experienced by some by discussing different aspects of lucid dreaming. The Lord isn't going to force any spiritual issues on us. Here is what I mean by that statement. He doesn't force us on matters of healing, deliverance, or prophecy. We must ourselves insist upon having these things, and at the very least opening our hearts to God to walk in the Spirit.

Working Towards a Definition

- What is lucid dreaming?
- How does it differ from the other types of dreams?
- How do we recognize a lucid dream?
- How often do lucid dreams occur?
- Can we really change the outcome of our dreams?

These are just some of the areas I hope to address in this chapter. I believe that as we focus on and begin to explore these topics it will awaken this aspect of dreaming for those that are interested (*1 Corinthians 12:1*).

We will also discuss the issue of dream incubation for Christians as well. I want to put the mind of the Christian at ease with this topic and others that we might have confidence and awareness of lucid dreaming and the techniques I will discuss and introduce here. I want to reassure those so concerned that God is foremost the Creator of the human mind and our sleep cycles, and any potential we have in our spirituality comes from Him, including lucid dreaming. God, in His omniscience, understands the human mind perfectly, and obviously better than any psychologist. Though counterfeits of lucid dreaming and dream incubation may exist, it is my conviction that we cannot react in fear. Prayerfully, let's move ahead into some new territory that many in the secular arena have called *lucid dreaming*.

Lucid- What Does it Mean?

Let's begin by looking at the term. What does this term "lucid" mean and where does it come from? It isn't a biblical term, so there must be some outside source that we can look to that will help us get a clearer idea of what is meant when people mention the concept of lucid dreaming. "Lucid", according to Webster's, is a term that means several things. Used as an adjective, it means "suffused with light: luminous". It also means "having full sense of one's faculties: sane." Thirdly, it is defined as "clear to the understanding: intelligible".

On the other hand, the term "lucidity" when used as a noun means "clearness of thought or style". Furthermore, it can be defined as "a presumed capacity to perceive the truth directly or instantaneously". All of this really gives us a framework to contemplate about the concept of a lucid dream.

It describes a dream that at least has the potential to be inundated and permeated with light, in which one has the full use of one's faculties (probably within the dream), which would include the use of our will or would involve our choices. We should all want more light in our lives and in our dreams. Light is good and comes from God. In fact, scripture tells us that God is light, and in Him there is no darkness (*1John 1:5*). This type of dream seems to be, at least by definition, a dream that has light and truth inherent in it. That's not all there is to it; let's continue to dig.

I really like the reference to saneness in these initial definitions. Psychologists and others have long thought that dreams are essential to health, wholeness and the overall well being of the psychological condition of an individual. Could it be that lucid dreams contribute to this "saneness" or wholeness in a person? Also it would seem to indicate that lucid dreaming brings some measure of clear understanding through the dream.

Wow, now that's incredible! I don't know about you, but I certainly want more light and truth, a sane and whole perspective and clear understanding through any means God will use to give it to me. Of course, we know it would most likely come from the Holy Spirit, since all God does is by His Spirit. Remember the word of the prophet Zechariah,

> *Not by might, not by power, but by my Spirit says the Lord.*
>
> *Zechariah 4:6*

The dream, even the lucid dream, comes from that same ancient, pure well and source. To qualify that statement, this does not mean that every lucid dream we hear comes from God.

We must discern the source of every dream, especially in this area of lucid dreams.

Some secular writers believe that the term and the roots of lucid dreaming were first used by Yogis in Tibet. Though that may be true for their historic studies and discoveries, I ultimately believe God is the author of lucid dreaming. The root of any capacity that we as a human race as descendants of Adam have for any such type of dream is derived from the Creator. If we are to truly give credit where credit is due, He is the one whom we can credit with this type of dream. If that is true, then perhaps we may find some scriptural basis. Here is an example to consider. Do you recall the dream that young King Solomon had after becoming king of Israel (*1Kings 3:5-15*)?

Could it be that the encounter Solomon had when the Lord appeared to him in his dream is a lucid dream account recorded in scripture? It is possible. The reason it is possible can be seen simply by the way Solomon responds to the question that came to him from the Lord. Therefore, by his response, he determined the outcome of the dream.

What if Solomon had responded differently? What if he would have asked, say for more governors, for the ruling of the kingdom? What if he asked for some other thing, such as riches, long life or health? It would have changed everything. But in the dream Solomon in his interaction with the appearance of the Lord asked for wisdom. We know the outcome of the account. The Lord was pleased with Solomon's request and granted it along with that which he did not request. All this wisdom may have been the fruit and outward sign of a lucid dream. The implications of this dream and its outcome are staggering. Though this particular dream may be classified as some other type of dream, I want to suggest that there was a lucid component to this experience of Solomon, at the very least.

Levels of Lucidity

Furthermore, in my experience, there seems to be different levels of lucidity. Many people that I have talked to, when interpreting dreams, share their experience of how they in some way were becoming aware that they could change their dream from within the dream. They were "awake" or in control to some extent in the dream, no matter how small that may be. It may be a flying dream for example, and learning how to fly or land within the dream. Some recognize that they have some level of control in their flying experience. This is one example of the beginning and the first sign that a dreamer is experiencing this type of lucid dream reality and the capacity to alter the outcome of the dream. It should be a signal to the dreamer that if they pay attention to this and develop it, they will be able to reach higher lucidity levels and gain even more control within the dream to determine its ultimate outcome.

How can this be useful to you and I as Christians? Why should we desire to work within our dreams in this way? Shouldn't we just go to sleep and if by chance we dream, then we allow the dream to take its own natural course? The answer is, "Yes, we should!" That is perfectly acceptable and something we all do, whether we are consciously aware of it or not. On the other hand, if at times we are able to change a dream from within, it will influence our waking hours. Solomon's dream produced eternal fruit and widespread renown in his life and for his God. Similarly, our ability to determine the outcome of our dreams will produce a desired result, rather than something void of God and His purpose and will for our lives. We are co-laborers with God and intricately involved with Him in His purposes, from the judging of angels, to judging the world, to being used by Him in His ministry of reconciliation. Why would it be difficult to grasp that God would give us such liberty in the workings of His Spirit in our dreams?

Dream Incubation?

Let's take a look at the practice of dream incubation.

- Can we induce a dream?
- Does this violate a spiritual principle?
- Does this type of practice cross over into the realm of the flesh or witchcraft?

Let's explore what dream incubation is, then let's see if there is a contradiction to this practice in scripture and its guidelines. What does scripture say and are we prohibited from this type of exercise?

Again, let's start with a definition of what "incubation" is. One definition is "to cause (as an idea) to develop". Another way we typically think of the term of incubation is in relation to the hatching of eggs and represents how the eggs are cared for through body warmth until they are ready to hatch; in other words, a preparation period.

This would mean then that the practice of dream incubation for Christians is that period of preparation prior to our sleep. It suggests that we need to prepare for sleep and that if we prepare properly, we will be more likely to dream, and possibly even enhance our lucid dream potential or capabilities.

Personally, I believe there are things we can and should do in order to prepare for sleep each night. As I grow older, the more I seek to enhance my night season and protect it as sacred and as a time when I will meet with God. This can happen through worship, prayer or through dreams and night visions. Every night therefore is holy and I will take measures to prepare myself to dream.

Some go as far as to assume that they can determine what they will dream. I don't agree with the notion that I can determine the topic of a dream, but rather this is an idea I guard against. It represents an illegal technique. This approach tries to induce something that does not have its origins in the will of God. We can ask God to speak to us through a dream about a particular subject, but ultimately our will must be submitted to His will and authority in our lives.

This idea of dream incubation that I am referring to is to focus or meditate on a given object or dream symbol, metaphor or scripture prior to sleep. This helps the dreamer signal to him or herself or in other words, it becomes a signpost within the dream. It helps one to realize that I am now dreaming and wanting to control the outcome of this dream to some good end. This is not selfish when seen in the correct light, but towards a selfless, godly and God directed end. Many will even have the experience of waking up from a dream and being unsatisfied with the result, so they go back to sleep and continue dreaming to change the outcome to their satisfaction. For our western mindsets this can be a stretch.

Some other ways we might consider preparing ourselves prior to bed would be to read scripture (see Chapter 2). Spending time in the Word of God and prayer before bed does a number of practical things. First, it brings us into the presence of God, which is where we need to be. In the presence of God we find His touch; the Spirit of God can bring peace. A second benefit to reading the Word of God prior to sleep is in the renewing of the mind and a great way to close our day. If we begin our day with God in devotion wouldn't it be wise to also end our day with some type of intimate time with Him as well?

Lucid dreaming is a fascinating aspect of the dreamer's repertoire of dreams as there are many types of dreams. Some are for healing, spiritual warfare, direction and guidance, and so on. It could be viewed as a tool in the vast tool chest of dreams and night visions. Lucid dreaming is valuable, as are all the other types of dreams that we receive from God. For the Lord to perform a particular function or purpose in our spiritual lives, we need different types of revelation (*1 Corinthians 12*). On one occasion, God may give a trance. On another occasion He may give us a vision. Furthermore, He may choose to give us a certain type of vision such as an open vision. Do you see where I am going with this? On different occasions, the Holy Spirit chooses according to His ways to show us things and do things in us for various reasons, and He can do this through a variety of means. My hope in introducing these concepts is not to make an exact science out of these types of revelation. By placing them in categories, we run the risk of putting them into our western worldview, which is closer to a Greek mindset. From the Hebrew or biblical perspective, these are hard to categorize, and there is overlap. My intention is simply to say that dreams are by the design of God a way that God chooses to speak to us. Lucid dreaming and Christ-centered dream incubation, though fascinating and powerful are tools that we as Christians can choose to embrace and consider as a piece of the bigger picture of understanding how God speaks to us in dreams and night visions.

Chapter 9
THE APPLICATION OF DREAMS–
I've Had a Dream from God, Now What?

One very important area to consider about dreams you receive from God is the application step of the process. What do I mean by an "application"? Here are a couple of definitions to consider.

An application is the act of applying; 1. An act of putting to use <application of new techniques> 2. A use to which something is put <new applications for old remedies> It is an act of *administering* or superimposing; another is *assiduous* attention. It can also be defined as a request or petition.

These are just some of the definitions for "application" and they help us to see that there's more to working with our dreams than we have previously thought. I want to raise our awareness of some principles of application and to gain a greater insight into the whole cycle of dreaming. This cycle has several parts including God, the dream itself, the interpretation, the application and its fulfillment.

I believe we are all in a place of growing in our understanding of how to respond to the revelation God gives to us. No one is perfect, and none of us have "arrived" yet in this process. Many issues need to be considered such as timing. We might ask God, "When will this come to pass?" or "When am I to deliver this revelation?" Scripture assures us that God gives grace to the humble (*James 4:6*). As we grow in faith, taking risks and even at times making mistakes in this area, God is using our very mistakes to help us mature and grow up in the Spirit.

Application Principle- Be Ye Doers...

Without knowing what to do, or put another way, knowing the application of a God given dream or vision, we fall short of the intent and purpose of God. We have to become aware of our responsibility when we are given revelation by the Holy Spirit. As with a prophetic word, a dream or a vision will often have conditions or a personal responsibility inherent within it that we must look to understand and act upon. How do we know what type of action is required from us is really the question at hand.

As a starting point and foundation for this aspect or step in the process, the book of James tells us we are to *"be doers of the word and not just hearers only, and thereby deceiving ourselves"(James 1:22).* We have noted before that it is important for us to respond to each dream, so what is it we must do? What does the dream require of us? Furthermore, what does God require of us in order for His will and purpose to occur in our lives, as a result of the dream.

Of course each dream will be different and is like a fingerprint or a human eye. Each has its own unique identity and characteristics. Though we may experience many dreams in a given category of dreams, such as healing dreams or spiritual warfare dreams they will all be a bit different in their application, so a one-type response that fits all is not going to necessarily work here. Always when dealing with dreams that are often so subjective and yet so distinctly from God, we need to guard against misinterpretation, which leads to misapplication. Not that it isn't okay to grow in our ability to interpret, which often implies making mistakes. God knows where we are in our growth process and will give us things in accordance with that process. This is not to say that we need to guard against misinterpretation with the intent of creating some legalistic fear in people but rather to establish better understanding and raise the level of sensitivity and our ability to hear the Spirit. I have seen and heard many people, including myself who reacted to a powerful dream rather than first praying and seeking the truth about its application. Its impact upon our spirit generates an urgency that we often don't know what to do with.

Many times when we receive a dream it will be very intense to us. Obviously this isn't always the case but it can be a life changing experience just to have a dream and not even know the interpretation. Think of Nebuchadnezzar who was so impacted by his dream and yet couldn't even remember it and demanded an interpretation along with the recounting of the dream or he would kill the wise men of his realm. This was a divine set up. Yahweh knew that Nebuchadnezzar's interpreters couldn't come up with the dream or somehow counterfeit this dream. He had deliberately hidden it from the King of Babylon in order to give the answer of the secret to Daniel.

Dream Sharing

Dreams and visions can even seem to come at a time when it is crucial for us to make important decisions in our lives. To make these major decisions in haste after having such a dream or vision may prove to be premature. We should be sure of an accurate interpretation first then after prayerful consideration and counsel to confirm our next steps, we then make any necessary changes in our lives. That may sound quite obvious but it is an issue that we can overlook. I do believe that dreams and visions are to be acted upon at some level, but with wisdom and faith that brings us closer to the will and the mind of God. This is one reason I believe that "Dream Guilds" or small groups that center on dream sharing are so vital to a healthy response. It gives us the objectivity that a growing believer needs by bouncing things off those who are likeminded in these small groups. It becomes an environment of truth and prayer. A Guild can be defined as "an association of people with similar interests or pursuits." It is in these Dream Guilds that we can find the truth we need from others in a safe environment and relational context.

Pitfalls and Prayer

One of the first pitfalls I have run into and would caution every dreamer about is this problem of not praying through a dream first before acting on it or sharing it with another. In an anxious and immature way we can be prone to making the wrong call or decision based upon a thing we think or assume the dream or vision is saying. I suppose this is nothing more than the process of maturation in relation to interpretive principles. It is a crucial area where we can hopefully minimize these mistakes by committing our dreams and our decisions to prayer. Some of us will learn this in the school of hard knocks and by making many mistakes as I have. This is okay if we understand the issue clearly; it can save us time and possibly years in the training process.

A given for us is that we need to always pray as a rudimentary, basic and proper response to any revelation given by God. I also suggest that when a person receives a dream or a vision to begin writing the revelation down (see Chapter 3 on Creative Journaling). This was the practice of the prophets of old and of Daniel who when he had a dream did the same. He wrote the dream down (*Daniel 7:1*). In essence what we are saying to God is that what He has spoken to us is important enough for us to get out of bed and write down what we just had a dream about. If it is difficult to write all the details, then simply write the main themes in the dream and it should serve to help you fill in the details later on when you are more coherent.

If we ignore the dream or revelation and thereby fail to value it by responding to it, we are in essence saying to God that what He is speaking isn't really all that important to us. It is essentially an attitude of the heart and a decision to make the effort to focus on the dream and to make room for it in our lives and busy schedules. We determine that attitude by our choice. Can you imagine saying to Almighty God, Creator of Heaven and Earth and things under the earth, that the dream He just gave to you isn't all that important? It is ludicrous. We may not be saying this directly, but our actions are saying it and our attitudes are saying it. God help us if we are in this place spiritually. It's one thing to not be sure if a dream is from God and another thing to immediately recognize that it is from God and not make some effort to respond and hear all that God is saying through that dream. We can change this by learning about proper responses to God and by making decisions to listen to His voice.

Another basic response to a dream and vision is to share it with a trusted friend or those gifted in the area to help interpret. Be sensitive to how the Holy Spirit may guide you to share things in a situation like this. You never know if you will meet the answer to your questions by listening to the Holy Spirit's prompting. It may be in a Dream Guild or small group setting that is formally arranged to share dreams. An answer may occur in the context of our everyday relationships. The Lord can use anyone anytime He desires to give you an insight or some answer to your prayer about a symbol or a dream. In any case, this can be a very surprising way that God will meet you if you are truly seeking an interpretation to a dream or a vision. To me this clearly represents the idea of body ministry and having healthy interdependence with other believers. God uses people and often chooses to speak to us through them. We need each other and even in this area of dream interpretation we can't be an island isolated and separate from others. I don't care how gifted a person is. Body life. This is the way that God has created us. We are to function within the framework of a people. The truth of the dream may not be fully revealed by these means but it can be of help in the search. Most friends will speak the truth even when it hurts so be prepared for what they may say and pray through their insight to make sure this is from God and not just their opinion. Judge, evaluate and weigh carefully their interpretation just as you would a prophetic word.

What Should I Begin to Pray About?

Here are some ideas as to how to pray. If there are specific people or places in our dreams then as a first level response we begin to pray for these people or places. We may not understand why they are in our dreams initially. It causes us to wonder if they are symbolic in some way or are they representing themselves in the dream. They may in fact be symbolic and we will get a clearer understanding by praying for them and by praying to understand why they appeared in the dream. This initial prayer will eventually cause us to dig deeper about the meaning.

Dreams are given in one sense to stimulate our relationship and intimacy with God and to help us understand Him and His ways. That is why we must lift our eyes to the God of Heaven for the answer to the dream's meaning and that is why the answers are often hidden. The Father desires an intimate relationship with each of us, and this is one way He draws us into that place of intimacy with Him. Learn not to lean upon the dream interpretive methods and focus on relationship with the author of the dream. He is the one who holds the full interpretation in His mind and His heart. Seek Him first and the interpretation and understanding of the symbols will come in time. You can be assured of that.

> *Ask and you will receive, seek and you will find, knock and the door will be opened.*
>
> *Mathew 7:7*

What About Dreams and Visions Training?

I need to qualify this statement. Training and equipping in this area is extremely important in clarifying interpretive principles and can be ultimately helpful but our answers *must* come from the Holy Spirit and from the mouth of the living God.

I look at this issue from the standpoint of some training that I had when I was studying music in college as a Jazz and composition major. Musicians where I studied were trained in theory, music history and in other traditional programs, but when it came to improvisation, which is a Jazz earmark, we had to in essence unlearn what we were taught and just learn to be musical. All the training in the world doesn't necessarily mean you will become musical. It comes from within. We had to learn to feel the rhythm and hear the lines in order to express the sometimes complex and higher level creativity that is deep inside a person.

It is a similar situation with dream interpretation. If we focus on only the training we will try to fit everything into the categories and systems of thought that we have been taught and begin to rely on that training rather than relying on and trusting the voice of God. He may have nuances to show us that color or shade the interpretation very differently than our traditional training. I'm not saying throw the training out. In fact, very few jazz musicians are untrained. I'm not saying you can't get there "by ear", but very few do so and the quality of your understanding and expertise expands with training. It builds a foundation upon which you firmly stand and walk. It isn't the whole building, rather just the foundation. But without a good foundation the building in the long haul is in trouble and won't withstand the changes that are inherent in the earth and ground. Training then is meant to prepare us for something. We don't stay in a place of training. We must go on from there. Though I thought many of my fellow college classmates seemed to make a career out of their college classes. It all must lead to something.

Do I Need to Change?

A second type of response after praying is to understand anything that is outlined in the dream as a condition. This points to some type of action that we must do in order for the fulfillment of the dream to take place. How can we know for sure if there is something that is required of us? Are there some dreams that are unconditional? The answer to these questions will become clearer as we take a look at dreams in scripture. Most dreams in scripture in fact were simply given and the outcome was predetermined; for instance when Joseph interpreted the dreams during his stay in the Egyptian prison. During this undesirable time in Joseph's life he interpreted the dreams of the chief Baker and the chief Butler of Pharaoh who were also his prison inmates. The interpretation Joseph gave stated the outcome, which was inherent in the dream, and it virtually could not be changed. The restoration of the chief Butler may have required his respect of Pharaoh and willingness to go back to his position of cupbearer, but it appears overall he wanted that anyhow. I'm sure the conditions of Pharaoh's court were much more to be desired than the prison. It may have cost him his life if he didn't respond and go back to his place in the court of Pharaoh. But the dream of the chief butler required nothing and could not be changed by anything this man could have done. His fate was sealed. He was to be hung and lost his life by the decision of Pharaoh and the dream revealed exactly that.

Other dreams though in fact did require a response. If you recall the dream of Joseph in the New Testament (*Mathew 2:13*), he was told by the angel to go to Egypt with the child Jesus and he and his wife Mary responded and did exactly as they were told. When they did this they remained safe from the murder that was intended of Jesus. It required an obedient response of the dreamer.

Chapter 10
REACHING PRE-CHRISTIANS
Through Dreams

In this chapter I want to explore the activity in the Holy Spirit in equipping Christians to interpret dreams and to minister prophetically to pre-Christians. From the onset of my journey in Christ, I was initially influenced by John Wimber's perspective of and a term he coined, Power Evangelism. In fact, the ministry of the Spirit and the works of God in power was the only reality I had known as a believer in my early experience. Prior to my conversion in my early 20's, I was not a church-goer. Life in the power of the Holy Spirit became normative for my church experience, as I knew it. Healings, miracles, deliverance, prophecy, dreams and the like were all part of the package of being a follower of Christ. Power evangelism was the natural outgrowth of using the power and gifts of the Holy Spirit as a means of impacting the lives of pre-Christians and advancing the Kingdom of God, outside the four walls of the church building. These influences were all part of my beginnings and the foundation of my life in God. As my process continued, I began to recognize that I had particular leanings in my relationship with God. I became more and more intrigued by the lives of the Old Testament prophets and the demonstrations of the Spirit revealed in their lives. Among the things that got my attention, I began to see in scripture how the Lord spoke to heathen kings and others who did not know Him by means of a dream. This has become much more of an issue to me over recent years of discovery. Let me explain how it has come to light.

In November of 1998 I moved from Southern California to Fort Worth, Texas in response to the voice and leading of God. Shortly after arriving, I was introduced to a Baptist church in Fort Worth. Like many churches in America, they had a home cell group system. After hearing about the home groups, the Lord spoke to me about starting a group focused on dreams. I consulted with a friend who also attended the church with his family and we began to plan the group as we discussed the vision and goals.

The group centered on dreams and interpreting that grew rapidly to the point that we were unable to stay in my friend's home. We decided to move it to accommodate the amount of people who were now attending weekly. The Lord graced our time and people were touched as several of us took a team leadership approach over the short life of the group. From within the group an idea surfaced that we should take dream interpretation into a local bookstore and set up a table to interpret dreams for the lost.

The bookstore received the idea with excitement and opened their doors once a month to our group. To my knowledge, this particular outreach met once a month in the same bookstore in Fort Worth, Texas, some years after it's initial start. This all began to reveal the heart of God to me for the lost, for those dreaming and seeking answers, in a way I hadn't previously known. As we began to answer their dilemmas and interact with people, their spiritual hunger became more evident and I began to see our culture and the opportunity before us in a way that I had not seen before.

Week after week, usually two or three times a week, for some three and a half years, I was out on the streets talking to people about their dreams and interpreting for the lost. I, along with others, did various event-oriented outreaches in locations such as Phoenix, Arizona, Atlanta, Georgia, San Diego, California and Houston, Texas to name a few. Through this whole process, the Lord created a fire in me to equip the church to interpret dreams, minister prophetically and by the power of the Holy Spirit, to advance the Kingdom of God in the lives of pre-Christians. I have also come to recognize that this is a great opportunity not only in our culture here in the United States, but also in many cultures around the globe.

This has been a brief description of my experience and as I have traveled, taught and talked with Christians about these types of opportunities; it is absolutely amazing to see their response when they hear about this type of evangelistic lifestyle. Early on, I simply wanted to help people understand their dreams and to share what little knowledge I had at the time within our small dreams home group. It was as though we stumbled into this opportunity. I found that it naturally fit the spiritual DNA that the Lord had given to many. He is developing leaders and the church to take this type of outreach effort on and continues to grow it in many places among diverse groups, ministries and church affiliations.

After much study, reflection and discussion, I now see in the scripture with a new lens those occasions when the Lord would speak to people who did not know Him or have a relationship with Him by means of a dream or vision of the night. The dreamer would often talk to a Joseph or a Daniel and receive the interpretation from someone who knew God and could speak and minister on His behalf and on behalf of the Kingdom of God. My experience has taught me that the Holy Spirit *is* being poured out (*Joel 2:28*) and as this happens, dreams are one of the things He releases. As with scripture, God is in the business of using the church to provide answers to the dreams he has given to pre-Christians. What an amazing plan! The God of Heaven speaks in the night and hides the meaning of the dream. He causes the one who receives the dream to seek for an answer and to find an understanding of what they experienced in order to relieve the intrigue that stirs within them.

Joseph Interprets Pagan Dreams

Let's look at an example of this type of activity in scripture to see how the Holy Spirit sets this up so wonderfully. I'm sure you recall the story of Joseph the favored son of Jacob, called a *dreamer* by his family, despised, envied and hated by those closest to him. Joseph found himself in prison after being falsely accused of an adulterous relationship with Potiphar's wife. In Genesis chapter 40, we read about these dismal circumstances of Joseph and the hardships he encountered to this point in his journey. One morning after waking up, two of his prison companions began to share the dreams they had the night before but were sad because they had no one to interpret the dreams and tell them what they meant.

There is a parallel here of a lesson we can learn as to what a dream without the meaning being revealed in a person's life and in our culture also cultivates. Their conversation with Joseph was interesting and revealing.

> *So he asked Pharaoh's officers who were with him in the custody of His Lord's house, saying, Why do you look so sad today? And they said to him, we have each dreamed a dream and there is no interpreter of it.*
>
> *Genesis 40:7*

What a profound statement that is and so many are saying the same thing today. If not verbally, they are saying it by going to the New Age interpreters or someone who is not of God.

These two men in prison were obviously not Christians or believers; they were those who stood in the court of an Egyptian King. They were as pagan as one could be, no doubt worshiping the gods of Egypt. But Joseph on the other hand was a devout Hebrew from the lineage and heritage of Abraham, Isaac and

Jacob his father. Jacob was also a dreamer, by the way (remember his encounter at Bethel where the angels were descending upon a great ladder and the Lord spoke to him from the top of it). The point is this; the Lord God gave these two men dreams in prison and knew very well they would not be able to understand them. He intentionally did this so that Joseph could interpret their dreams knowing that one day he would be restored to greatness and a place of influence through the favor of God. The omniscient God would one day use him to bring redemption to the nation of Egypt by means of the dreams given to Pharaoh. The ways of God are high and we see them in action here in Joseph and in his unpleasant circumstances. What his brothers meant for evil, God meant for good. Yahweh had Joseph just where He wanted him. There is much to learn from Joseph when we begin to consider the realm of dream interpretation. Let's continue on.

Joseph responds and speaks to the two men with complete confidence in his God, "Do not interpretations belong to God? Tell them to me." I love his response. His trust was completely in Yahweh and not in any other man alive or any other interpretive method he might have learned from the Egyptians. Remember, Egypt was steeped in a belief that dreams were significant and were to be heeded. We now have come to understand how important of a role dreams played in the Egyptian culture through papyrus and inscriptions found in modern excavations by archeologists. They too believed, as did the Hebrews, that these dreams contained messages of importance. It is even thought by some that dream interpreters were of a high status within Egyptian culture.

So it was with Joseph, and so it should be with us. Let me explain. When we as believers have been equipped and hear the dream of a pre-Christian, we too can have great confidence that the meaning of the dream is completely understood by the one who lives within us, if we are born again and filled with the light of God. Joseph took great delight in understanding the dream and telling them the meaning, though one of them was quite difficult news to tell. The result of this interaction is fulfillment. The dreams came to pass just as Joseph interpreted them. One man was restored to his position in Pharaoh's court and the other was hung on a tree and lost his life. The two dreams both foretold their future and it was accurately understood and revealed by the interpreter Joseph. God was with Joseph and here is compelling evidence of the Kingdom of God at work even in dismal circumstances.

Divine Appointments

This brings up the issue of divine appointments. Divine appointments are those occasions when God will set up, as it were, an encounter or relationship that is meant in His plan to bring about His intended purpose. Have you ever met or talked with someone and knew that it was supposed to take place and orchestrated by the hand of God? That is a divine appointment. Divine appointments can be seen in the life of Joseph as with these two men in prison. He was set up by the Lord to help them understand their dreams and they were set up by the Lord to receive the dreams and therefore need an understanding. It was all for the glory of God and His ultimate purpose in the bigger picture. It was all brought about completely by His Spirit. We merely avail ourselves as his vessels as did Joseph. The big picture was obviously restoring Joseph and the Hebrews, the covenant and later the Messiah who came from this profound lineage. But the immediate picture took one step at a time, which first came through the interpreting of these two Egyptian's dreams in prison and later Pharaoh's dreams.

In our outreaches I have heard on numerous occasions people make statements to the effect that convinced me that God had led them to our dream interpretation tables. When we make a commitment to be at a given location month in and month out and are faithful, the Lord seems to give pre-Christians dreams because He knows they will come across our path. I hear things like this; "It's amazing that I had this dream last night and now you guys are right here tonight!" This tips me off immediately that it is a divine set up. God wanted them to come to us and speak about their dreams. Often other issues of life come up because the dream generally ties to an important and intimate detail of their circumstances and relationships. The implications of this are quite profound. Once a person has opened up to share their dream, they will often feel safe enough to share other things about themselves as well.

This helps us build relationships with them and we can offer help in time of crisis or in times of need. This is where the local church comes in. We can invite them or offer assistance in a relational context. The Holy Spirit will minister to some people in power on the spot, but others we will begin to build a bridge into their lives on a continuing basis.

One thing leads to another. Once people begin to discuss their lives, we are listening to them and the Holy Spirit. In this context, words of knowledge and prophetic words begin to flow and the light of the Holy Spirit surrounds the time. It is quite an exciting dynamic that keeps one pressing into God and listening to His voice.

I believe this type of evangelistic effort that involves dream interpretation, prophecy and other gifts of the Spirit have just begun to emerge in the body of Christ. Many are in the process of becoming aware they have a gift to interpret while others are practicing and gaining confidence and maturing in their understanding. My experience is that every time we go out into a public forum we learn new things about how to do this type of outreach better. We also deepen in our understanding of the important social and spirituality issues of our day that are quite unique to all of history. I believe this type of ministry has potential to be revolutionary in nature for the body of Christ. It is not a cliché to say that everyone dreams. Therefore, in time, even the most conservative evangelicals will be forced to look at this issue more closely. Dreams are undeniable in scripture and not only for the believer but also for the unbeliever. We have a harvest to reap and an unquestionable opportunity to do it in a culturally relevant way by the power of the Holy Spirit. God help us as we grow in our effectiveness in this area of ministry!

Chapter 11
DREAMS:
A Doorway to the Supernatural

The supernatural expression of God is a very real aspect of Christ-centered spirituality that beckons our attention and understanding in order to be relevant in today's culture. We are seeing the rise of the supernatural in many places today. Why then is the church largely silent on this issue? Our fears seem to cause us to shy away from anything that could possibly deceive us and unfortunately we close our eyes and ears to the cry of the world that is searching with a great hunger for the true supernatural experience and power of God. We as the church hold the key to this reality being shown and displayed just as Moses and Aaron demonstrated the superior power of God over the counterfeit of Pharaoh's magicians (*Exodus 7:11*). I am convinced that the true light and the true supernatural that is in Christ is certain to emerge as we *grow* in the Spirit in the coming years and decades (*Romans 8*). Dreams and visions are a doorway to the supernatural that we are invited to participate with God in His works and activity in the earth today. Let's take a look at some of the ways that this is being revealed and manifested in our times.

Many things can occur in dreams and night visions that stretch our limited human minds and reasoning. From day to day we live in the reality of the physical, empirical world of our senses and we are comfortable with rational thinking. We live within the framework of the laws of creation and the numerous dimensions such as length, height, width, depth, time and space. We interact with our world and our universe as we know it, but some dreams and visions seem to defy many of the known and accepted dimensions.

Flying Dreams

For instance, have you ever had a flying dream? If you haven't, let me briefly illustrate this. It is a fairly common type of dream where often a person will be literally flying without the assistance of any other outside source. It will feel exhilarating to many, and is usually quite enjoyable. Of course everyone has different scenarios within the context of a flying dream. This is just one type of scenario that one may encounter in a flying dream.

Dreams, as we have discussed, are very personal and so it is with flying dreams. For instance, I recall a flying dream that I had one night while living in Southern California. I was flying and enjoying my wonderful flight time and then suddenly out of nowhere a known prophet appeared in the dream. He was flying not far away from me singing a song. This prophet is a robust man, and it looked quite hilarious and I laughed and felt so much joy as he smiled at me in flight. He went past me and was displaying a similar prowess in mid-air, as if to encourage me. I didn't have wings or wasn't on a jet in this instance, nor was the jovial prophet; we were flying in mid air.

These types of dreams defy what our minds are unable to allow for because of the natural laws we understand and normally operate under. Furthermore our flesh is at enmity with our spiritual life. Faith is the key to unlocking this. The flying dream for example allowed me to experience freedom in flight when mankind and my flesh would tell me that we as mere mortals couldn't fly because we aren't birds with wings, but we are two legged human beings with real physical limitations. I'm grateful for people like the Wright brothers who in the early 1900's didn't believe that either. In other words, the dream and what I experienced broke all the known and accepted scientific rules and the laws of nature. Perhaps this is why dreamers are quite different than most people in how they view reality and in the way they think creatively.

Night Travel and Time Travel

Another way that dreams may defy the known dimensions is by night travel. Night travel might be described as when a person experiences a sense that in the dream or the vision they have been taken to another location or place. It feels as if they were really taken to another geographical area for a purpose that the Spirit of God has in mind in this particular occasion. Why couldn't this happen? After all, God is omnipresent and to think that He might take our human spirit to another location and then return us in a dream is not unfathomable. This type of experience is not uncommon to those in church history nor is it unusual to the dream experience in other cultures, which further verifies to me the validity of the experience. In the experiences I have had with this, it was as if I was *really* in the location. When I awoke, I *knew* I had been in the particular place that I was taken in order to receive and hear the message and to have the encounters I was to have. All of this was to accomplish the will and purpose of the Father.

This experience of travel in dreams may not only include travel in terms of geographical change, but also this can occur to transcend the dimension of time. God seems to use dreams and visions to take us forward in time to see the future. This also is not inconsistent with the theology of God being the Eternal and Omniscient God. In His infinite and higher ways He chooses to reveal things of this nature to His friends.

Spiritual Warfare and Dreams

Dreams, as I have mentioned, seem to break all the rules. They also serve to warn us about the evil supernatural forces at work in the world. Spiritual warfare dreams are another type of dream that help us to see and deal with these enemies of Christ and His body. It is as though the Lord pulls back the veil and allows us to understand what are their planned attacks, purpose and activity. This puts our national intelligence agencies to shame in comparison. God is infinitely more aware and knowledgeable of the bigger picture. This is of course very sobering to most of us, but something we must be alert to or we are just beating the air with our traditions. How do we fight effectively a war in the Spirit? More importantly, how do we fight the battles that are presently before us seeing that final outcome of the war has been won at the cross of Jesus Christ?

It is essential for us to be alert and one way we are awakened to our enemy and his camp is through dreams and night visions. Any military strategist will tell you that in order to fight successful battles you must know your enemy and his weaponry. Through dreams we can see the specific areas that the evil one is targeting and seeking to destroy. We can also see it from God's perspective and not through the eyes of fear or idealism. There is so much for us to learn from God in dreams about this war and conflict between the kingdom of light and kingdom of darkness. We can't afford to be lulled back to sleep any longer if we are to effectively resist and overcome the enemy and his tactics.

Often the things in the natural speak to us of the things going on in the spiritual ream. For instance, we in the United States have lived with a false sense of security for some time. With the attacks of September 11th we have been awakened to a real enemy and those who vehemently despise our nation and the ideologies we stand for. Here is the thing we keep hearing coming out of the State Department and that is, we must not be lulled into believing that the war on terror is over. On the contrary, the enemy is waiting for an opportune time to advance and to strike again when we are unsuspecting and where we are weakest or have let our guard down and are left vulnerable.

I see a parallel here with the church. We have lived largely with a false sense of security for a long time. We have been attacked and at times rather harshly and we have paid dearly and have lost loved ones. We run the risk of being lulled back into the attitude that everything seems to be fine for now, but in reality, we are still at war.

Satan in Cleric's Garb

Let me give you a shocking example of a dream I had that frightened me out of my sleep one night. This dream revealed what the enemy was doing in the midst of an evangelistic dream interpretation outreach. We experienced a wonderful time talking mostly to the youth this particular night. I was quite excited by the things we were seeing the Holy Spirit doing by giving accurate interpretations to dreams, prophecy and words of knowledge for the lost by our team.

These youth were obviously touched by the Holy Spirit and we were building relationships with them. When I went home that night I went to sleep and had a dream. In the dream I saw myself talking on a cell phone to an attractive gentleman somewhere in his early to mid 50's. He was balding, and I noticed that he was wearing light brown or tan priest's clothing that had the traditional white "dog collar" as they are affectionately called by some. I was talking to this man on the cell phone from some distance and yet at the same time I was seeing him in the dream. Instantly I knew in the dream that this man was evil and although he looked attractive and religious I was aware that he had evil intent. He began to speak clearly about his plan for those who were involved on the evangelistic dream interpretation team that night at the outreach. One by one, he spoke of his plan for each of their lives.

Immediately I awoke and needless to say, I was terrified. I was not talking to some ordinary demon like gossip or lust, or one that harasses people insidiously. This evil figure had disguised himself as a religious cleric and furthermore was very attractive to the eye. I knew his plans in a very clear way and began to intercede for those who I was responsible for in this dream outreach.

These types of things are never pleasant to talk about and even as I write about this incident, I have no desire to get our focus on the wrong place. We need to hear God's voice in dreams about spiritual warfare in order to overcome the attacks and the malevolent intent of the enemy. The Lord will give us wisdom to fight the good fight with weapons that are not carnal, but spiritual.

> *For the weapons of our warfare are not carnal, but mighty through God to the pulling down of strongholds.*
>
> *2 Corinthians 10:4*

Dreams are an aspect of that weaponry in our arsenal that has been at the very least forgotten or belittled in importance by many.

The way I responded to this dream was to intercede for the people who were involved in ministry with me. I prayed and asked the Lord to stop these attacks. I did not begin pulling down principalities or the religious spirit over this geographical area. The result of this dream burned in me a truth and a lesson I will never forget. It raised my awareness of the spiritual reality we face in this type of evangelistic ministry situation with the gifts of the Holy Spirit, including the prophetic and dream interpretation. We were taking back coveted ground the enemy has had in this area of the Spirit for possibly decades, centuries or even longer. He has deceived even the elect as it were by portraying to many that dreams and dream interpretation are things that belong in the occult and not in the church. By us being open to the Holy Spirit night after night in the outreaches we are taking back what belongs as part of the inheritance of the people of God and establishing a stronghold of God in that community. All Satan does in this realm is to counterfeit and destroy through his false interpreters such as mediums, psychics or other New Age people.

Revelation is very powerful and especially when used to win the lost. It exposes the enemy and moves the people into the presence of God quickly. It can come in a dream interpretation or a word of knowledge or by a prophetic word or other such manifestations of the Holy Spirit. The lost and those seeking will hear His voice and experience His presence giving them light, hope and guiding them into a relationship with the Creator. People in our culture and in this time in history are longing for this true expression of the Ancient of Days and the God of Heaven. We must understand the fight that the enemy will give to steal this gift away from us and at the very least to resist our efforts.

Dreams, Angelic Messengers and Scripture

Although we have introduced the role of angels I want to develop this idea more. Angels play a prominent role in scripture. They appear at pivotal places and times to accomplish the divine will. They appear not only in the Old Testament covenant community, but they also appear in the life of Jesus and the early New Testament church. It seems that in our "advanced "culture we have lost the sense of our need for angels and the angelic host. Furthermore, we seem to have lost the understanding of the important function they play in our personal lives and in the life of the church. Why this has subtly taken place over time is a debate and I suppose there are many theories and some speculation, but the point being that we are gaining new perspective of the angelic role in our generation. We are being visited again and receiving the angels with welcome and open hearts to their message and to their presence. How can we possibly live without them?

Dreams and visions often are filled with these heavenly beings to help us carry out the divine mandate for our ministries and callings. Our effectiveness depends on their help and aid. They are those created to assist in the divine order of things on the earth and in heaven. As in scripture the angels take on different forms and appear in different ways. I suppose this has to do with their level of authority, purpose and the type of angel that is appearing. In any case, this is an aspect of the supernatural in God that is being revealed in dreams and visions. Again, the veil is drawn back and we begin to recognize that they are at work in a particular situation and they are powerful, having significant roles and messages that we must hear and pay attention to if we are wise.

Let's take a look at the connection of dreams and angelic activity in scripture that will be a basis for what I am hoping to communicate in this section. I intend also for this to expand our ideas about how God uses dreams and the angelic that are part of His ways in the Spirit. We must remember that God who is Spirit is a supernatural being and He often uses supernatural means to accomplish His purpose. This is who He always has been, and this is what He has always done, but because of the philosophies of our age and in this post-modern era we have reduced Him to something less than whom He is, to our own demise.

If you recall the account of Jacob and the dream He experienced at the place he called Bethel, or the house of God; Jacob had an encounter with Yahweh and with the angelic at what he described as the "gateway of heaven" (*Genesis 28*). On this night like many other nights, Jacob went to sleep under the open starry skies. Using a rock as his headrest or pillow he dozed of to blissful sleep. During the night he sees in his dream a tall ladder that reached to the heavens where angels were ascending and descending. Angelic activity in this location was prolific and unhindered. They seemed to freely move down and up in that geographical location with ease and frequency and it further sounds as if there were many angels using this tall ladder or staircase that Jacob describes. I can almost picture the intense activity of these messengers of light quickly moving about unhindered by our worldly dimensions. An open heaven might be an appropriate term to use here. Jacob without intent was led to an open heaven. Jacob wasn't searching for this but rather it was as if he stumbled into it or was led by the Lord to this spiritual goldmine that later amazed him when he says, "Surely God is in this place and I did not know it" (*Genesis 28:16*).

The story continues where the Lord God appears to Jacob at the top of the ladder reaching to the heavens as if peering down to him. What an incredible occasion. The Lord God appears to his chosen servant in a dream. This is of course not the only time we see this type of thing happen in scripture where through a dream the Lord God appears. This wasn't some obscure instance or impression, but the living God appeared in a dream.

It is hard to imagine what Jacob felt as he awoke that morning. I'm sure it etched the fear of the Lord in his mind like little else would and served to change the rest of his life. Furthermore, the covenant between Israel and Yahweh was renewed in this dream. Amazing, isn't it? Not only was this a supernatural encounter with the angelic host of heaven, but it was also an encounter with the Lord of Hosts speaking and appearing, renewing the covenant giving promise both to Jacob and to his descendants. It doesn't get much better than that.

What Do Angels Look Like?

We don't get much of a description of these angels ascending and descending on this heavenly staircase. Where scripture is silent we must be careful to not read more into it than we see plainly. In other angelic occurrences in scripture we know more about how they appeared both openly and in dreams. For instance, in some cases, angels appeared as men. These heavenly beings were given an ability to be among human beings to accomplish their mission on earth and appear in a different form than their normal heavenly bodies and glory. Interesting, isn't it? In some dreams, we too can encounter people that are heavenly messengers. Like the scripture, they appear human but they are not. They come in all shapes and sizes, colors and races. If it seems rather strange to you when you have a person that you do not know and therefore do not understand why they are in your dream, this may be explained as the appearance of an angel. Of course the truth of the issue and the interpretation of the dream will be revealed by the Holy Spirit as you begin to pray and search for the answer.

Index

SCRIPTURE REFERENCES

Dreams and Night Visions in Scripture

Old Testament

Abimelech's Warning Dream:

Genesis 20:3-7

*3 But God came to Abimelech in a dream by night, and said to
him, Behold, thou art but a dead man, for the woman which thou hast
taken; for she is a man's wife. 4 But Abimelech had not come near her:
and he said, Lord, wilt thou slay also a righteous nation? 5 Said he not
unto me, She is my sister? and she, even she herself said, He is my
brother: in the integrity of my heart and innocency of my hands have I
done this. 6 And God said unto him in a dream, Yea, I know that thou
didst this in the integrity of thy heart; for I also withheld thee from
sinning against me: therefore suffered I thee not to touch her. 7 Now
therefore restore the man his wife; for he is a prophet, and he shall pray
for thee, and thou shalt live: and if thou restore her not, know thou that
thou shalt surely die, thou, and all that are thine.*

Jacob's Dream of the Cattle:

Genesis 31:10-13

10 *And it came to pass at the time that the cattle conceived, that I*
lifted up mine eyes, and saw in a dream, and, behold, the rams which
leaped upon the cattle were ringstraked, speckled, and grisled. 11 *And*
the angel of God spake unto me in a dream, saying, Jacob: and I said
here am I. 12 *and he said, lift up now thine eyes, and see, all the rams*
which leap upon the cattle are ringstraked, speckled, and grisled: for I
have seen all that Laban doeth unto thee. 13 *I am the God of Bethel,*
where thou anointedst the pillar, and where thou vowedst a vow unto
me: now arise, get thee out from this land, and return unto the land of
thy kindred.

Laban's Dream:

Genesis 31:24

24 *And God came to Laban the Syrian in a dream by night, and said unto him, Take heed that thou speak not to Jacob either good or bad.*

Joseph's Dream of the Sheaf:

Genesis 37:5-8

[5]And Joseph dreamed a dream, and he told it his brethren: and they hated him yet the more. [6]And he said unto them, hear, I pray you, this dream which I have dreamed: [7]for, behold, we were binding sheaves in the field, and, lo, my sheaf arose, and also stood upright; and, behold, your sheaves stood round about, and made obeisance to my sheaf. [8]and his brethren said to him, shalt thou indeed reign over us? or shalt thou indeed have dominion over us? And they hated him yet the more for his dreams, and for his words.

Joseph's Dream of the Sun, Moon and Stars:

Genesis 37:9-10

[9]And he dreamed yet another dream, and told it his brethren, and said, Behold, I have dreamed a dream more; and, behold, the sun and the moon and the eleven stars made obeisance to me. [10]and he told it to his father, and to his brethren: and his father rebuked him, and said unto him, what is this dream that thou hast dreamed? Shall I and thy mother and thy brethren indeed come to bow down ourselves to thee to the earth?

The Dream and the Interpretation of the Chief Butler:

Genesis 40:5-13

5*And they dreamed a dream both of them, each man his dream in
one night, each man according to the interpretation of his dream, the
butler and the baker of the king of Egypt, which were bound in the
prison.* 6*And Joseph came in unto them in the morning, and looked
upon them, and, behold, they were sad.*7*And he asked Pharaoh's officers
that were with him in the ward of his Lord's house, saying, Wherefore
look ye so sadly to day?*8*And they said unto him, We have dreamed a
dream, and there is no interpreter of it. And Joseph said unto them, do
not interpretations belong to God? tell me them, I pray you.* 9*And the
chief butler told his dream to Joseph, and said to him, In my dream,
behold, a vine was before me;* 10*And in the vine were three branches:
and it was as though it budded, and her blossoms shot forth; and the
clusters thereof brought forth ripe grapes:*11*And Pharaoh's cup was in
my hand: and I took the grapes, and pressed them into Pharaoh's cup,
and I gave the cup into Pharaoh's hand.* 12*And Joseph said unto him,
This is the interpretation of it: The three branches are three days:*13*Yet
within three days shall Pharaoh lift up thine head, and restore thee
unto thy place: and thou shalt deliver Pharaoh's cup into his hand,
after the former manner when thou wast his butler.*

The Dream and Interpretation of the Chief Baker:

Genesis 40:16-19

16When the chief baker saw that the interpretation was good, he
said unto Joseph, I also was in my dream, and, behold, I had three white
baskets on my head: 17And in the uppermost basket there was of all
manner of bakemeats for Pharaoh; and the birds did eat them out of the
basket upon my head.18And Joseph answered and said, This is the
interpretation thereof: The three baskets are three days, 19yet within
three days shall Pharaoh lift up thy head from off thee, and shall hang
thee on a tree; and the birds shall eat thy flesh from off thee.

Pharaoh's Two Dreams:

Genesis 41:1-4

1And it came to pass at the end of two full years, that Pharaoh
dreamed: and, behold, he stood by the river. 2And, behold, there came
up out of the river seven well favoured kine and fatfleshed; and they fed
in a meadow. 3And, behold, seven other kine came up after them out of
the river, ill favoured and leanfleshed; and stood by the other kine upon
the brink of the river. 4And the ill favoured and leanfleshed kine did eat
up the seven well favoured and fat kine. So Pharaoh awoke.

Genesis 41:5-8a

5And he slept and dreamed the second time: and, behold, seven
ears of corn came up upon one stalk, rank and good.6And, behold, seven

thin ears and blasted with the east wind sprung up after them. 7And the seven thin ears devoured the seven rank and full ears. And Pharaoh awoke, and, behold, it was a dream. And it came to pass in the morning that his spirit was troubled.

Joseph Interprets Pharoah's Dreams:

Genesis 41:25-32

25And Joseph said unto Pharaoh, The dream of Pharaoh is one: God hath shewed Pharaoh what he is about to do. 26The seven good kine are seven years; and the seven good ears are seven years: the dream is one. 27And the seven thin and ill favoured kine that came up after them are seven years; and the seven empty ears blasted with the east wind shall be seven years of famine. 28This is the thing which I have spoken unto Pharaoh: What God is about to do he sheweth unto Pharaoh. 29Behold, there come seven years of great plenty throughout all the land of Egypt: 30And there shall arise after them seven years of famine; and all the plenty shall be forgotten in the land of Egypt; and the famine shall consume the land; 31And the plenty shall not be known in the land by reason of that famine following; for it shall be very grievous. 32And for that the dream was doubled unto Pharaoh twice; it is because the thing is established by God, and God will shortly bring it to pass.

The Midianites Dream and Interpretation, Gideon:

Judges 7:13-15

13 *And when Gideon was come, behold, there was a man that told a*
dream unto his fellow, and said, Behold, I dreamed a dream, and, lo, a cake
of barley bread tumbled into the host of Midian, and came unto a tent, and
smote it that it fell, and overturned it, that the tent lay along. 14 *And his*
fellow answered and said, This is nothing else save the sword of Gideon the
son of Joash, a man of Israel: for into his hand hath God delivered Midian,
and all the host. 15 *And it was so, when Gideon heard the telling of the*
dream, and the interpretation thereof, that he worshipped, and returned
into the host of Israel, and said, Arise; for the Lord hath delivered into your
hand the host of Midian.

Solomon's Dream:

1Kings 3:5-15

5 *In Gibeon the Lord appeared to Solomon in a dream by night:*
and God said, Ask what I shall give thee. 6 *And Solomon said, Thou*
hast shewed unto thy servant David my father great mercy, according
as he walked before thee in truth, and in righteousness, and in
uprightness of heart with thee; and thou hast kept for him this great
kindness, that thou hast given him a son to sit on his throne, as it is
this day. 7 *And now, O Lord my God, thou hast made thy servant king*
instead of David my father: and I am but a little child: I know not how
to go out or come in. 8 *And thy servant is in the midst of thy people*
which thou hast chosen, a great people, that cannot be numbered nor

counted for multitude.9Give therefore thy servant an understanding heart to judge thy people, that I may discern between good and bad: for who is able to judge this thy so great a people? 10And the speech pleased the Lord, that Solomon had asked this thing. 11And God said unto him, Because thou hast asked this thing, and hast not asked for thyself long life; neither hast asked riches for thyself, nor hast asked the life of thine enemies; but hast asked for thyself understanding to discern judgment; 12Behold, I have done according to thy words: lo, I have given thee a wise and an understanding heart; so that there was none like thee before thee, neither after thee shall any arise like unto thee. 13And I have also given thee that which thou hast not asked, both riches, and honour: so that there shall not be any among the kings like unto thee all thy days. 14And if thou wilt walk in my ways, to keep my statutes and my commandments, as thy father David did walk, then I will lengthen thy days. 15And Solomon awoke; and, behold, it was a dream. And he came to Jerusalem, and stood before the ark of the covenant of the Lord, and offered up burnt offerings, and offered peace offerings, and made a feast to all his servants.

Nebuchadnezzar's Dream of the Great Image:

Daniel 2:1

1And in the second year of the reign of Nebuchadnezzar Nebuchadnezzar dreamed dreams, wherewith his spirit was troubled, and his sleep brake from him.

Daniel 2:19

19Then was the secret revealed unto Daniel in a night vision. Then Daniel blessed the God of heaven.

Daniel 2:28

28But there is a God in heaven that revealeth secrets, and maketh known to the king Nebuchadnezzar what shall be in the latter days. Thy dream, and the visions of thy head upon thy bed, are these; 29As for thee, O king, thy thoughts came into thy mind upon thy bed, what should come to pass hereafter: and he that revealeth secrets maketh known to thee what shall come to pass. 30But as for me, this secret is not revealed to me for any wisdom that I have more than any living, but for their sakes that shall make known the interpretation to the king, and that thou mightest know the thoughts of thy heart. 31Thou, O king, sawest, and behold a great image. This great image, whose brightness was excellent, stood before thee; and the form thereof was terrible 32This image's head was of fine gold, his breast and his arms of silver, his belly and his thighs of brass, 33His legs of iron, his feet part of iron and part of clay. 34Thou sawest till that a stone was cut out without hands, which smote the image upon his feet that were of iron and clay, and brake them to pieces. 35Then was the iron, the clay, the brass, the silver, and the gold, broken to pieces together, and became like the chaff of the summer threshing floors; and the wind carried them away, that no place was found for them: and the stone that smote the image became a great mountain, and filled the whole earth.

Daniel Interprets Nebuchadnezzar's Dream:

Daniel 2:36-45

36This is the dream; and we will tell the interpretation thereof before the king. 37Thou, O king, art a king of kings: for the God of heaven hath given thee a kingdom, power, and strength, and glory. 38And wheresoever the children of men dwell, the beasts of the field and the fowls of the heaven hath he given into thine hand, and hath made thee ruler over them all. Thou art this head of gold. 39And after thee shall arise another kingdom inferior to thee, and another third kingdom of brass, which shall bear rule over all the earth. 40And the fourth kingdom shall be strong as iron: forasmuch as iron breaketh in pieces and subdueth all things: and as iron that breaketh all these, shall it break in pieces and bruise. 41And whereas thou sawest the feet and toes, part of potters' clay, and part of iron, the kingdom shall be divided; but there shall be in it of the strength of the iron, forasmuch as thou sawest the iron mixed with miry clay. 42And as the toes of the feet were part of iron, and part of clay, so the kingdom shall be partly strong, and partly broken. 43And whereas thou sawest iron mixed with miry clay, they shall mingle themselves with the seed of men: but they shall not cleave one to another, even as iron is not mixed with clay. 44And in the days of these kings shall the God of heaven set up a kingdom, which shall never be destroyed: and the kingdom shall not be left to other people, but it shall break in pieces and consume all these kingdoms, and it shall stand for ever. 45Forasmuch as thou sawest that the stone was cut out of the mountain without hands, and that it brake in pieces the iron, the brass, the clay, the silver, and the gold; the great God hath made known to the king what shall come to pass hereafter: and the dream is certain, and the interpretation thereof sure.

Nebucadnezzar's Night Vision; the Great Tree:

Daniel 4:10-17

*10Thus were the visions of mine head in my bed; I saw, and behold
a tree in the midst of the earth, and the height thereof was great.11The
tree grew, and was strong, and the height thereof reached unto heaven,
and the sight thereof to the end of all the earth:12The leaves thereof were
fair, and the fruit thereof much, and in it was meat for all: the beasts of
the field had shadow under it, and the fowls of the heaven dwelt in the
boughs thereof, and all flesh was fed of it. 13I saw in the visions of my
head upon my bed, and, behold, a watcher and an holy one came down
from heaven; 14He cried aloud, and said thus, Hew down the tree, and
cut off his branches, shake off his leaves, and scatter his fruit: let the
beasts get away from under it, and the fowls from his branches:
15Nevertheless leave the stump of his roots in the earth, even with a
band of iron and brass, in the tender grass of the field; and let it be wet
with the dew of heaven, and let his portion be with the beasts in the
grass of the earth: 16Let his heart be changed from man's, and let a
beast's heart be given unto him; and let seven times pass over him.
17This matter is by the decree of the watchers, and the demand by the
word of the holy ones: to the intent that the living may know that the
most High ruleth in the kingdom of men, and giveth it to whomsoever
he will, and setteth up over it the basest of men.*

Daniel Interprets Nebuchadnezzar's 2nd Dream:

Daniel 4:19-27

19Then Daniel, whose name was Belteshazzar, was astonied for one hour, and his thoughts troubled him. The king spake, and said, Belteshazzar, let not the dream, or the interpretation thereof, trouble thee. Belteshazzar answered and said, My Lord, the dream be to them that hate thee, and the interpretation thereof to thine enemies. 20The tree that thou sawest, which grew, and was strong, whose height reached unto the heaven, and the sight thereof to all the earth; 21Whose leaves were fair, and the fruit thereof much, and in it was meat for all; under which the beasts of the field dwelt, and upon whose branches the fowls of the heaven had their habitation: 22It is thou, O king, that art grown and become strong: for thy greatness is grown, and reacheth unto heaven, and thy dominion to the end

of the earth. 23And whereas the king saw a watcher and an holy one coming down from heaven, and saying, Hew the tree down, and destroy it; yet leave the stump of the roots thereof in the earth, even with a band of iron and brass, in the tender grass of the field; and let it be wet with the dew of heaven, and let his portion be with the beasts of the field, till seven times pass over him; 24This is the interpretation, O king, and this is the decree of the most High, which is come upon my Lord the king: 25That they shall drive thee from men, and thy dwelling shall be with the beasts of the field, and they shall make thee to eat grass as oxen, and they shall wet thee with the dew of heaven, and seven times shall pass over thee, till thou know that the most High ruleth in the kingdom of men, and giveth it to whomsoever he will. 26And whereas they commanded to leave the stump of the tree roots; thy kingdom shall be sure unto thee, after that thou shalt have known that the heavens do rule. 27Wherefore, O king, let my counsel be acceptable unto thee, and break off thy sins by righteousness, and thine iniquities by showing mercy to the poor; if it may be a lengthening of thy tranquillity.

Daniel's Night Vision of the Four Beasts:

Daniel 7:1-14

1In the first year of Belshazzar king of Babylon Daniel had a dream and visions of his head upon his bed: then he wrote the dream, and told the sum of the matters. 2Daniel spake and said, I saw in my vision by night, and, behold, the four winds of the heaven strove upon the great sea. 3And four great beasts came up from the sea, diverse one from another. 4The first was like a lion, and had eagle's wings: I beheld till the wings thereof were plucked, and it was lifted up from the earth, and made stand upon the feet as a man, and a man's heart was given to it. 5And behold another beast, a second, like to a bear, and it raised up itself on one side, and it had three ribs in the mouth of it between the teeth of it: and they said thus unto it, Arise, devour much flesh. 6After this I beheld, and lo another, like a leopard, which had upon the back of it four wings of a fowl; the beast had also four heads; and dominion was given to it. 7After this I saw in the night visions, and behold a fourth beast, dreadful and terrible, and strong exceedingly; and it had great iron teeth: it devoured and brake in pieces, and stamped the residue with the feet of it: and it was diverse from all the beasts that were before

it; and it had ten horns. 8I considered the horns, and, behold, there came
up among them another little horn, before whom there were three of the
first horns plucked up by the roots: and, behold, in this horn were eyes
like the eyes of man, and a mouth speaking great things. 9I beheld till
the thrones were cast down, and the Ancient of days did sit, whose
garment was white as snow, and the hair of his head like the pure wool:
his throne was like the fiery flame, and his wheels as burning fire. 10A
fiery stream issued and came forth from before him: thousand
thousands ministered unto him, and ten thousand times ten thousand
stood before him: the judgment was set, and the books were opened. 11I
beheld then because of the voice of the great words which the horn
spake: I beheld even till the beast was slain, and his body destroyed, and
given to the burning flame. 12As concerning the rest of the beasts, they
had their dominion taken away: yet their lives were prolonged for a
season and time. 13I saw in the night visions, and, behold, one like the
Son of man came with the clouds of heaven, and came to the Ancient of
days, and they brought him near before him. 14And there was given him
dominion, and glory, and a kingdom, that all people, nations, and
languages, should serve him: his dominion is an everlasting dominion,
which shall not pass away, and his kingdom that which shall not be
destroyed.

New Testament References

Joseph's Dream:

Mathew 1:20

20But while he thought on these things, behold, the angel of the Lord appeared unto him in a dream, saying, Joseph, thou son of David, fear not to take unto thee Mary thy wife: for that which is conceived in her is of the Holy Ghost.

The Wise Men's Warning:

Mathew 2:12

12And being warned of God in a dream that they should not return to Herod, they departed into their own country another way.

Warning to Flee to Egypt:

Mathew 2:13

13And when they were departed, behold, the angel of the Lord appeareth to Joseph in a dream, saying, Arise, and take the young child and his mother, and flee into Egypt, and be thou there until I bring thee word: for Herod will seek the young child to destroy him.

Direction to Return to Israel:

Mathew 2:19-20

*19But when Herod was dead, behold, an angel of the Lord
appeareth in a dream to Joseph in Egypt, 20saying, arise, and take the
young child and his mother, and go into the land of Israel: for they are
dead which sought the young child's life.*

Warning of Archelaus' Reign in Judea:

Mathew 2:22-23

*22But when he heard that Archelaus did reign in Judaea in the
room of his father Herod, he was afraid to go thither: notwithstanding,
being warned of God in a dream, he turned aside into the parts of
Galilee 23and he came and dwelt in a city called Nazareth: that it might
be fulfilled which was spoken by the prophets, He shall be called a
Nazarene.*

Pilate's Wife's Warning:

Mathew 27:19

*19When he was set down on the judgment seat, (Pilate) his wife
sent unto him, saying, Have thou nothing to do with that just man: for
I have suffered many things this day in a dream because of Him.*

Paul's Night Vision:

Acts 16:9-10

And a vision appeared to Paul in the night; There stood a man of Macedonia, and prayed him, saying, Come over into Macedonia, and help us. And after he had seen the vision, immediately we endeavoured to go into Macedonia, assuredly gathering that the Lord had called us for to preach the gospel unto them.

Miscellaneous References to Dreams

Deuteronomy 13:1-5:

[1]If there arise among you a prophet, or a dreamer of dreams, and giveth thee a sign or a wonder, [2]And the sign or the wonder come to pass, whereof he spake unto thee, saying, let us go after other gods, which thou hast not known, and let us serve them; [3]Thou shalt not hearken unto the words of that prophet, or that dreamer of dreams: for the Lord your God proveth you, to know whether ye love the Lord your God with all your heart and with all your soul. [4]Ye shall walk after the Lord your God, and fear him, and keep his commandments, and obey his voice, and ye shall serve him, and cleave unto him. [5]And that prophet, or that dreamer of dreams, shall be put to death; because he hath spoken to turn you away from the Lord your God, which brought you out of the land of Egypt, and redeemed you out of the house of bondage, to thrust thee out of the way which the Lord thy God commanded thee to walk in. So shalt thou put the evil away from the midst of thee.

Numbers 12:6-8:

6And he said, Hear now my words: If there be a prophet among you, I the Lord will make myself known unto him in a vision, and will speak unto him in a dream. 7My servant Moses is not so, who is faithful in all mine house. 8Wwith him will I speak mouth to mouth, even apparently, and not in dark speeches; and the similitude of the Lord shall he behold: wherefore then were ye not afraid to speak against my servant Moses?

1 Samuel 28:6:

6And when Saul enquired of the Lord, the Lord answered him not, neither by dreams, nor by Urim, nor by prophets.

1 Samuel 28:15:

15And Samuel said to Saul, Why hast thou disquieted me, to bring me up? And Saul answered, I am sore distressed; for the Philistines make war against me, and God is departed from me, and answereth me no more, neither by prophets, nor by dreams: therefore I have called thee, that thou mayest make known unto me what I shall do.

Job 4:12-17:

12Now a thing was secretly brought to me, and mine ear received a little thereof. 13In thoughts from the visions of the night, when deep sleep falleth on men, 14fear came upon me, and trembling, which made all my bones to shake. 15then a spirit passed before my face; the hair of

*my flesh stood up 16it stood still, but I could not discern the form
thereof: an image was before mine eyes, there was silence, and I heard a
voice, saying, 17shall mortal man be more just than God? shall a man
be more pure than his maker?*

Job 20:8:

8He shall fly away as a dream, and shall not be found: yea, he shall be chased away as a vision of the night.

Job 33:14-17:

*14For God speaketh once, yea twice, yet man perceiveth it not.15In
a dream, in a vision of the night, when deep sleep falleth upon men, in
slumberings upon the bed; 16then he openeth the ears of men, and
sealeth their instruction, 17that he may withdraw man from his
purpose, and hide pride from man.*

Psalm 73:20:

20As a dream when one awaketh; so, O Lord, when thou awakest, thou shalt despise their image.

Ecclesiastes 5:3:

[3]*For a dream cometh through the multitude of business; and a fool's voice is known by multitude of words.*

FOR MORE INFORMATION

For more information about Prophetic Innovations training events and resources, visit the web site at:

www.WhatEveryDreamMeans.com

E-mail: info@WhatEveryDreamMeans.com

Following is a list of dreams training events available from Prophetic Innovations:

Level 1 Dreams Seminar

Lifestyle Foundations for Dreams and Visions

Level 2 Seminar

Interpreting Dreams and Visions

Level 3 Dreams Seminar

Practical Dream Interpretation

Dreams Seminar

Dream Interpretation in the Marketplace